My good friends Ken and Trudi Blount have written a book on marriage and the family that raises the bar on producing a successful family in Satan's world. It's one of th[illegible] is never too late to take heed to Go[illegible] in His Word. Problems and mistak[illegible] continual theme of the book. The au[illegible] family life, which makes the book au[illegible] just theological. It was written just for you.

—Bob Yandian
Author and international evangelist
Former pastor of Grace Church
Tulsa, Oklahoma

Devil-Proof Your Family is a must-read for everyone. Ken and Trudi present biblical truths that they have shared over the last thirty years in their ministry to children and moms and dads. This is sound, biblical teaching on how to have a strong family and raise your children so they have a Christian foundation for life. I have known Ken and Trudi for over thirty years and have seen firsthand how they devil-proof their family with the Word of God. Today, their children and grandchildren are serving God and are examples of how this book can devil-proof your home.

—Jay Roberson
Senior pastor, Tascosa Road Fellowship
Amarillo, Texas

I wish every human being alive could read Ken and Trudi Blount's new book, *Devil-Proof Your Family*. For over forty years I have been ministering among God's people globally and preaching just about every day of the week. I can't help but notice the severe warfare and attack against families. This book will arm you, it will equip you, and it will anoint you to deal with the invisible enemy soldiers (demons) that are trying to steal your children, ruin your marriage, and pollute your home. I believe this book is an absolute necessity for the survival of families in these last days. God is still God, His Bible is still the truth, and His presence is the only thing that destroys the yoke and lifts the burden—which is what will happen to you as you read each page of this powerful new tool the Blounts have provided by the power of the Holy Spirit.

Ken and Trudi, job well done! I hold you in high esteem, and I thank God for your work in the body of Christ. May this book be anointed and reach multitudes, in Jesus's name.

—Mark T. Barclay
Preacher of Righteousness
Mark Barclay Ministries

Ken and Trudi Blount have been mandated by God to rescue and empower today's family. In their book, *Devil-Proof Your Family,* the Blounts call on years of practical experience and an unquestionable Holy Spirit unction to unveil what far too many families don't know: "There is a real devil, and he is out to destroy your home."

With scriptural support and divine insight, Ken and Trudi bring a timely message that carries a prophetic anointing. This is a must-read for parents or grandparents (or potential ones) who want to ensure the spiritual protection and success of their families. You will find the information practical yet biblical, current yet timeless!

—Tom Turner
Lead pastor, Praise Family Church
Mobile, Alabama

Every generation experiences the need for relevant truth. In their new book, *Devil-Proof Your Family,* Ken and Trudi Blount share truth and revelation from God to this current generation. The Blounts' wisdom comes from decades of experience in multiple areas coupled with their deep knowledge of the Word of God.

Many public figures present a pre-programmed image for the public. However, I have known the Blounts for many years, and Ken and Trudi are the real deal. They not only teach truth, but they have implemented these truths in their own lives.

In their new book, they meticulously walk you through the principles of how to devil-proof your family and back up each truth with Scripture. Whether your family is in total disaster or it seems like everything is going well, this book will be a lifeline of wisdom as you apply these God-ordained principles in your life. They are life-changing and can heal a broken family. I highly recommend *Devil-Proof Your Family*.

—Dr. Larry Ollison
President, International Convention
of Faith Ministries
Osage Beach, Missouri

Family is the foundation of society, and Ken and Trudi Blount are God-given specialists in sharing truths which bring strength and stability to that foundation. The message they share is not simply a theory but a lifestyle they have proven out in their own lives. For the pastor in need of a tool for his church, for the family or marriage going through a difficult time, for the person who just wants to grow in relationships, this book is definitely for you!

—Mark Brazee
Pastor, World Outreach Church
President, Domata International School of the Spirit
Tulsa, Oklahoma

DEVIL-PROOF YOUR FAMILY

KEN & TRUDI BLOUNT

Devil-Proof Your Family by Ken and Trudi Blount
Published by Charisma House
Charisma Media/Charisma House Book Group
600 Rinehart Road
Lake Mary, Florida 32746
www.charismahouse.com

Design Director: Justin Evans

Visit the author's website at https://kenblountministries.com.

Library of Congress Cataloging-in-Publication Data
Blount, Ken.
Devil-proof your family / by Ken and Trudi Blount. -- First edition.
pages cm
Includes bibliographical references.
ISBN 978-1-62998-628-9 (trade paper) -- ISBN 978-1-62998-629-6 (e-book)
1. Families--Religious aspects--Christianity. 2. Families--Religious life. 3. Marriage--Religious aspects--Christianity. 4. Spiritual warfare. I. Title.
BV4526.3.B65 2015
248.4--dc23
2015025198

First edition

15 16 17 18 19 — 987654321
Printed in the United States of America

DEDICATION

We dedicate this book to our children, Kari Brooke Blount Sparkman and Joshua Ryan Blount. You were our life projects (guinea pigs), but by God's Word and His grace you have turned out to be two of the most amazing people and best friends we have on the earth. We love you.

CONTENTS

ACKNOWLEDGMENTS

TRUDI AND I want to acknowledge and thank almighty God for the Bible, His holy Word. We have endeavored to carefully base every principle we teach on what we have learned from the Bible and not just our own good ideas.

We have experienced firsthand in our family that God's Word will never fail, no matter what challenges we experience. It may not be easy, but the patient application of God's Word into the battles of life will bring about change, no matter how impossible the situation may seem.

Jesus came for the purpose of transforming our lives and enabling us to overcome our sin and reverse the curse that it produced. The virtue to do this is found in His Word. We pray that as you read this book, the principles we lay forth from His Word will empower you to change your family...forever.

FOREWORD

THIS BOOK IS written by a couple who have devoted their lives since salvation to the cause of Christ—not just in ministry but in every area. As their son, I lived under the principles written in this book, and I can tell you they have left a lasting mark on my life. I was not a child who upon reaching adulthood had to overcome the shortcomings of my upbringing. In fact, on the contrary, I feel my upbringing played like a slingshot that launched me into many of the successes and the favor I am walking in today.

Part of my parents' legacy is this. At every major stage of my life, as I looked at the horizon of my future, I aspired to live up to the standard that was placed before me in my upbringing. On my wedding day, on the days my children were born, in victory and in devastation, I have always reflected on the consistent pattern that was modeled in the home I was privileged to grow up in.

My parents, like any parents, were not perfect, and they are transparent enough to make that clear in this book. But I always knew where they stood. They stood with Jesus, they stood united as a married couple, and they stood for me.

They are, in this writer's opinion, a model of the biblical parenting style. They were consistent in love, open, and honest. When I was growing up, they were my cheerleaders, coaches, and standard-bearers. They were involved and helped me understand the greater spiritual truths that are at work in this fallen world. They protected me yet they didn't shelter me.

They fought for me and they taught me how to fight. They taught me that I can have anything Jesus has for me, but it's not automatic. I will have to fight the devil for it and take it by force! The same is true for you today. You can have anything the Bible says you can have, but the devil will not give up an inch except by force.

Not fighting is not an option. If you choose not to fight, the enemy of your life will not choose to take it easy on you. No, he will clean your clock!

There is a powerful, abundant life possible for you and your family, but it lives on the other side of a battle. I know this because my very existence, the life I live, was made possible because of a fight! My mother was barren; she couldn't have children (you'll read more about that in the pages to come). But my parents sided with God's Word, stood in faith, and fought for me, and because of it I exist today. My life was made possible because a couple made the decision to fight the enemy's attempts to rob them of children!

I can't help but wonder as I write this what life might be possible for you if you will just fight for it. I know this: the life you dream of is possible. But make no mistake about it, you will have to fight for it.

If you want an incredible, godly marriage and kids who don't depart from the things of God when they grow up, if you want to be the spiritual leader of your home, you can have it. But you will have to fight for it, and this book will show you how. It will help you strategize and partner with God so you can fight to attain all that He desires for your marriage and family.

We are called to be fighters. All the victory in your marriage and family has already been won for you through the completed work of the Cross. You can't take any of your wealth or material possessions with you when you die. But if you will partner with Jesus and do all you can to stand, you will find yourself one day in heaven with the only ones you can take with you—your family. I can think of no greater achievement.

We win when we fight. We win when we stay aggressive. So choose to be a fighter, choose to partner with Jesus, and choose to outwork, outfight, outlast—out-anything—the devil.

Fight the good fight for your family! It's worth it.

—Joshua Blount
Pastor, New Song Church
Oklahoma City, Oklahoma

Introduction

WE ARE IN A WAR

THERE IS A battle raging for the hearts and minds of people in our day that is unprecedented in human history. The real enemy behind this war is not a political system or a concept such as moral relativism. Our adversary is an invisible, evil genius that is strategizing a vast plan and directing every step. His name is the devil.

The devil is real. He is not an abstract idealism or a doctrine. He is an angel created by God who fell from his exalted position in heaven and now inhabits the spiritual atmosphere of planet Earth.

The devil's stock-in-trade is deception. That's what he used to trick Adam and Eve in the Garden of Eden. The deception he sold them led to mankind's fall from grace and the subsequent curse that came on the earth. This curse is the reason for every wicked and dark thing we see taking place in our time. The Bible tells us, "We don't want to unwittingly give Satan an opening for yet more mischief—we're not oblivious to his sly ways!" (2 Cor. 2:11, THE MESSAGE).

The devil is evil but he is not stupid. His design is to steal from people, try to kill every person he can, and utterly destroy every human being on the planet (John 10:10). He really does hate people and he plays for keeps.

I'm not trying to glorify the devil or his power, but I want you to be fully aware of the situation we all face. If we want a strong marriage and children who love God and fulfill their purpose in life, we have to come to terms with the fact that *we are in a war.*

In the beginning stages of World War II when Hitler and his Nazi regime began their march through Europe, people underestimated their power. Hitler began in Poland, quickly overpowering the towns and villages in what became famous as blitzkrieg warfare.

Hitler's troops came with no fanfare or warning, and people had no idea what was happening or what they were facing. They were caught completely off guard. The Nazis would roll into town with soldiers, guns, and tanks, and the people were so unprepared they would try to oppose them with rocks and shovels. They had no chance and were utterly demolished. It was no contest at all, because these nations were not equipped for the battle.

I am convinced that one of the biggest issues plaguing Christians today is that we are not equipped to wage war against our enemy, the devil. The Apostle Paul instructed, "Finally, my brothers, be strong in the Lord and in the power of His might. Put on the whole armor of God that you may be able to stand against the schemes of the devil" (Eph. 6:10–11, MEV). Why would we need armor if there was no threat?

We are in a battle. There is no escaping it. There is no going AWOL. We are in a fight to the finish, a life-or-death conflict.

The enemy wants to *destroy you and your family.* And every day he plots and schemes how to do it. He has plans, tricks, tactics, and a team of demons working round-the-clock looking for ways to get at you. He knows, as pastor Tony Evans once said, that whoever controls the family controls the future.[1]

Make no mistake: this war is not going to disappear until Jesus returns. If you don't show up ready to fight, you're going to lose. And in the world today, there are a lot of people who are losing. They lose because they don't understand that they are in a war. They lose because they don't understand who the war is against. They lose because they don't understand where the battle is being fought. They lose because they don't understand who is against them, and most importantly they lose because they don't understand who is for them.

Our marriages can be strong. Our children can love God and be on fire for Him. We can protect our homes from the attacks of the enemy. But this victory won't be handed to us on a silver platter. We must go to battle.

The devil hates us. He's a bully and a cheater. He's sneaky and deceptive. He doesn't play fair, and he doesn't back off or show mercy. He doesn't take it easy on the weak or the young. He is every awful, ugly, horrible thing that exists.

But here is a great truth: Satan's a mean bully, yes. But *we have an ally on our side*. His name is Jesus.

The devil hates us so much because God loves us so much. The devil is really angry with God. Ever since God threw Lucifer out of heaven all those years ago, the enemy has been trying to get back at God by attacking what God loves the most—His children.

Satan's attacks against you really should be like an alarm clock going off, reminding you of the Father's love.

God loved us so much that He allowed His Son to be born into this fallen earth to rescue us from the scourge of sin. God was willing to stoop down to our level, get in the middle of our mess, and clean it all up for us. Jesus didn't come and just throw us a life raft. The Cross shows us that He dove right into the middle of our mess. When we call out to Jesus for help, He grabs us and pulls us to safety—if we will let Him.

God got it all back

Adam's sin affected all mankind and produced the curse of sin and death, but the one it affected the most was God. The fall of mankind meant God lost His family.

God made the earth for people, because He wanted to reproduce Himself. Simply put, He wanted a family. God wanted people to be born in His likeness so that we could walk with Him, love Him, and reproduce ourselves, because He wanted children.

When mankind rebelled against God, it severed the relationship He could have with His family. God, who is holy, could no longer have close fellowship with the children He had made. He had to distance Himself from the family He had created and loved.

The separation that now existed could not be fixed by man. Adam and Eve were evicted from paradise (the Garden of Eden), because they had to be separated from the presence of God.

The Bible says God "drove out the man" from the Garden of Eden (Gen. 3:24, KJV). The Hebrew word translated "drove out" here is *garash*, which can also mean "divorce." The separation that now existed between God and Adam and Eve was like a divorce. Because of their rebellion He had no other choice.

Anyone who has been divorced knows it is one of the most painful experiences anyone can have. It is a tearing apart of something that was at one time spiritually and emotionally joined. A pastor once used this analogy for divorce: "Picture two pieces of paper glued together; now try to separate them. What happens? Both papers tear apart."[2]

God knows firsthand the pain and despair of divorce. He knows it because He has been through it. In dealing with the subject of divorce in Malachi 2:16, God declared that He hates "putting away" (KJV), or divorce. Some have interpreted that verse to mean God hates those who have gone through divorce.

Wrong interpretation. God doesn't hate people. God hates divorce because of how much divorce hurts people. God loves people and hates for them to hurt.

That is why He sent His Son. Through His death on the cross, Jesus came to fix the separation between God and man and reconnect us to our Father. He came to heal the wounds caused by sin. And He came to give us back the authority we lost in the garden.

When Jesus died on the cross, He triumphed over the enemy. He got back—in full—everything that was lost when Adam and Eve fell. He got it *all* back! Colossians 2:15 says, "Having disarmed principalities and powers, He made a public spectacle of them, triumphing over them in it." This means we can have victory in our families. We can walk in unity with our spouse, enjoy the time we spend together, and raise children who serve and honor God. It means single parents can raise children who defy all the negative statistics about kids who grew up in one-parent homes.

We can do this because Jesus already gained the victory over the enemy. But we have to lay claim to that victory.

Too many Christians are losing their marriages and their children to the enemy because they don't know who they're up against or how to fight him. That's why we have written this book, to equip you for the battle.

In this book we will show you practical principles from Scripture that, when applied, will thwart the enemy's attacks against your house. Notice I didn't say these principles would stop the attacks against your family. As long as you live in the earth you will have to deal with the enemy's aggression, but you don't have to succumb to it. Our goal is to show you how to put up barriers now that will repel future attacks the enemy will wage against your home.

We will share from our experience and from our years

ministering about marriage and family issues in churches across the nation. If anyone had the odds stacked against them to have a long-term marriage and raise a successful family, it was us. We grew up in a small farming community in the sixties and were only nineteen and seventeen years old when we got married. We heard rumors that people around town were saying, "Those two will never make it."

People had reason to say that. Besides being very young, we knew little about life and less about how to connect in our marriage. We loved each other but didn't know how to live with each other. After being married for just a few months it seemed we were constantly fighting. But a miracle happened. We both met Jesus and our lives were turned upside down, or should I say right side up.

Even after we were saved, we still didn't know how to get along, but we had a heart to learn. Because of our commitment to be involved in a local church, study God's Word, and never quit, our marriage has endured. We have been married for forty-four years now and have two children and five grandchildren (so far) who love God and are committed to serving Him.

Our life has not been perfect. We have taken some hits along the way and made some mistakes. The enemy has tried to kill Trudi on two separate occasions, but we experienced the miraculous power of Jesus and she was healed. There are some things that have happened that we still don't understand and probably won't this side of heaven. But we have learned that when disappointments come, there is always a new day and new grace in Jesus.

This book is about cooperating with God and allowing Him to work in and through you. It is about recognizing that God loves you and is for you and your family. It is about using the authority you have been given in Christ to recover what the enemy has stolen from you and then shutting the gate so he can't do it again.

If you are a single parent or married to someone who doesn't share your desire to devil-proof your family, don't worry. This book is for you too. The strategies outlined in these pages will help equip any spouse or parent to protect your home from the enemy's attacks, regardless of your situation.

You will notice that this book is cowritten by Ken and Trudi Blount. Although I (Ken) am doing the writing, all of the research and organization was done in partnership with Trudi. In fact, Trudi is the one who dug up most of the spiritual secrets from the original Hebrew text. But this book shares our story and the things we have learned and teach together in our ministry.

The principles to build a successful marriage and raise children who love God are established early on in the Bible. Much of what we will share in these pages is actually based on the first three chapters of Genesis, which contain powerful revelation about the family. We are also going to discover some of the secrets about God's heart concerning family that are encoded in the original Hebrew, the language in which the Old Testament was written.

I pray what you learn in the pages of this book will reveal the heart of God to you and give you the ammunition you need to devil-proof your family for a bright and powerful future. So let's get started by going back to the beginning.

PART I

A BREACH IN THE HEDGE

Chapter 1

YOUR SPIRITUAL SECURITY SYSTEM

YOU CAN NEVER really understand God until you understand family. He created the earth because He wanted a family. He is a God of love, and He created people so He could express and share His love. Family is everything in the heart of God.

There is a principle in Bible interpretation called the law of first mention. This is the idea that the first mention or occurrence of a subject in the Bible gives us an idea of its significance throughout all of Scripture and how it is viewed by God.[1] This law lets us know the subject remains unchanged in the heart of God throughout Scripture. With this in mind, let's look at Genesis 1.

After God created the earth as we know it, He declared, "Let us make man [meaning man and woman] in our image, after our likeness, and let them have dominion [the ability to rule and make decisions]" (Gen. 1:26, MEV). Then in verse 28, He tells them to be fruitful and multiply, which means He wanted them to reproduce themselves. God's entire plan revolved around the creation of families. And the law of first mention lets us know that God's heart about family doesn't change throughout Scripture. Families are central to His eternal plan.

Even the language of the Bible points to the importance of family. The Old Testament was written in Hebrew, which is a very expressive language. There are twenty-two letters in Hebrew and unlike in English each letter has a numerical value and a word picture, or a concept, that corresponds with the letter. When the different letters and concepts are put together, they tell stories and principles about God.[2]

The very first letter of the entire Bible (not the first word, the first letter) is the Hebrew letter *bet*, which corresponds to our English letter B. The Hebrew symbol, or the word picture, for the letter *bet* is a house. Most of the time in Scripture, when you see the word house, you can substitute it for the word family. So the entire Bible begins with a letter depicted by a house, a word that often means family in the Bible. I don't think that is a coincidence. God's original intent in the beginning—the reason He created the earth—was to have a *family*. Family is the foundation for everything He did. He is a God of love, and He created people so He could express and share His love. Family is everything in the heart of God.

Family is also a major theme in Scripture—perhaps *the* major theme. After the creation of the earth, there was a marriage of the first two people created. Then Scripture ends in the Book of Revelation with the marriage supper of the Lamb. So the Bible begins with a wedding (Adam and Eve becoming one) and ends with a wedding (the Bridegroom returning for His bride, the church). The story in between is about a Father birthing a family, seeing family dysfunction and loss, then working for centuries to get His family back. (He finally succeeds in the end!) Because of the importance God placed on family, it was the first thing Satan attacked.

Keeping the garden

After God created man from the dust of the ground but before Eve came on the scene, God did two things. He gave Adam a place to live then He gave him an assignment, or a job.

> Then the Lord God took the man and put him in the garden of Eden to till it and to keep it.
>
> —Genesis 2:15, MEV

Adam's assignment was twofold. He was to "tend" the garden. This means he was the caretaker. You could even say he was a farmer. But there was another part of his job.

Adam was to "keep" the garden. The word "keep" here actually means he was to protect, guard, and keep watch over it. Why would God tell Adam to protect the garden? Because there was a danger of someone intruding. A closer look at the Hebrew meaning of "Garden of Eden" gives insight into God's command.

The word "Eden" comes from the Hebrew letters *ayin* (eye or to see), *dalet* (door, pathway), and *noon* (activity, life) and can be interpreted to mean eternal life.[3] It must have been a virtual paradise. God placed man in this wonderful place to enjoy a perfect life of provision, health, and protection. Mankind was supposed to walk with God in this perfect place and enjoy life at its best. Now add to that the fact that the word translated "garden" in Genesis 2 doesn't just mean a pretty place where plants grow. It also means an enclosure or hedge.[4] So when we put the words together, we see that "Garden of Eden" means a hedge of eternal life.

The word translated garden (*gan*) suggests there was a barrier or a fence around this wonderful paradise. Part of Adam's job was to keep any intruder or trespasser from coming across the property line. This is because God knew there was an intruder that would try to cross Adam's property line and invade the garden.

Adam was supposed to use the authority God had placed in his hands to keep the enemy (the serpent) out of the garden. Adam was supposed to devil-proof the garden God gave him and his family. It was part of his job description. God told him in Genesis 1:28, "Be fruitful and multiply, and replenish the earth and subdue it. Rule over the fish of the sea and over the birds of the air and over every living thing that moves on the earth" (MEV).

Notice the verse says mankind was to "subdue" and "have dominion" over the earth. This dominion was to be exercised as man walked in partnership with God. In a partnership each party has a role to play. Man's part was to protect the garden, using his God-given dominion to subdue the earth. God's part was to use His awesome power to back the man up as He obeyed His Father.

Think about this like a security system you install in your home. Trudi and I have a wonderful home filled with all kinds of electronics, family pictures, furniture, and many other things we cherish. We have spent several years and thousands of dollars turning our house into the nice home it is today.

Our house means a lot to us so we protect it, and we have many different lines of defense for our home. We have locks on our doors and windows and a security system that is monitored twenty-four hours a day. The monitoring company works with us much like God works with people. The company backs us up to protect us from invasions. They will alert the police, who will show up with force if there is any kind of breach in the perimeter.

Our security system has sensors and motion detectors as well as fire and carbon monoxide alarms. If we set the alarm and a door opens, a big bull horn begins to sound and the security system notifies the monitoring company. If no one turns it off, the police are sent. We are set up to be protected.

But our security system doesn't just keep bad things out; it also keep the good things in. We can set our security system to chime when a door or window opens. Why? Because we have a pool, and we need to know if one of our little grandkids goes outside because we wouldn't want one of them to fall into the pool with no one around.

All of these things are a part of our line of defense. We're not living in fear of bad things happening, but we're being safe and smart. We want to protect the things we care about, and we have many different tools to help us do that.

God's security system is no different. He uses many different lines of defense and has given us authority over the enemy so we can keep ourselves protected.

So here is the truth. In the Garden of Eden man didn't do his job. When the serpent came along that day and invaded his property line, Adam should have immediately evicted him. It was in his authority to do so. Adam could have said, "Whoa! Who are you and why are you on my property? You can just leave the same way you entered. Get out!" If Adam had done that God would have backed him up, and the enemy wouldn't have stood a chance. But Adam did not do his part. He was passive and it cost him everything.

You may be wondering, "Why didn't God intervene and kick the serpent out Himself?" If you've ever asked yourself that, what I am about to say is very important for you to understand. God had delegated that authority to Adam, and God is true to His word. He had given Adam authority to guard the garden, and He was not going to take it back. The fact of the matter was Adam didn't fulfill his part of the bargain, and God couldn't do it for him.

The Bible tells us, "Now the serpent was more cunning than any beast of the field" (Gen. 3:1). The serpent came to tempt. His goal was to deceive Adam and take what didn't belong to him, and he was very tricky in his approach. When the devil comes against people he always does it seductively. The Bible calls Satan an "angel of light" (2 Cor. 11:14). Light catches a person's attention and fascinates. The devil draws people with "lights" that look good on the surface but will ultimately wreak havoc in our lives. He speaks to our head (he always comes with enticing thoughts) and makes things that will destroy our life look "shiny" and inviting. Remember, the devil only has one goal, and that is to take you for everything you have!

The devil's objective in the garden was to get inside the property line and sell his bag of goods to Adam and Eve. The devil wanted to create a wedge between Adam and Eve and entice them into disobeying God. It is very interesting that we have no evidence of the serpent coming around when Adam was alone in the garden. But as soon as the woman came on the scene and they married, we have the first record of his appearance. He saw this marriage as a threat, so he came to destroy it in its infancy. I believe the devil's greatest fear is a marriage that honors God.

You know what happened next—the deal with the forbidden fruit. Eve was seduced. Adam should have evicted the serpent, but he didn't. Instead, he and Eve allowed a breach in the hedge and laid down the authority God had placed in their hands. The devil didn't attack Adam and Eve straight up. He deceived them into choosing to sin.

Doors wide open

I can have the greatest security system in the world, but if I go on a trip and leave the doors of my house wide open and the security system turned off, what good will it do me?

If something has been stolen when I return after a few days, I can't call up my security company and complain that their system didn't work. The theft was my fault, not theirs. I left the door open. I didn't follow the stipulations of the contract I signed with them. Simply put, I didn't do my part.

Satan is real. He hates all of us, and he will do anything he is allowed to do. It's not just by chance that we have troubles and struggles. It's because we have an enemy that is actually fighting against us. The Bible warns us, "Be sober and watchful, because your adversary the devil walks around as a roaring lion, seeking whom he may devour" (1 Pet. 5:8, MEV).

God tells us in this verse that we need to keep our guard up because our enemy is looking to devour us. We need to keep the windows and doors to our lives and families locked so Satan can't get in and steal the things God has blessed us with. Remember, Satan doesn't leave us alone because we're Christians. On the contrary, that makes him try that much harder to steal the things that God has for us.

But notice 1 Peter 5:8 uses the term "may." It says the devil is seeking whom he "may" devour. This means he is looking for someone who will give him permission. He has to get your cooperation before he can come in and wreck your life.

How does he get permission? He gets permission through sin and any other open doors. Satan is watching us, constantly looking for a chance to steer us away from God. He is looking for any little opening he can find to get in and mess things up in our lives. He wants to wreck your family with disunity, loss of intimacy, hurt and unforgiveness, rebellion, disrespect, promiscuity, and the like. And when we sin or fail to safeguard ourselves, our relationships, and our children from his attacks, we leave ourselves wide open for him to come in and steal from us.

Sin is just the opening Satan needs to get in and mess things up for you, so you have to cut the sin out. Before you can even think about protecting your marriage and your family from Satan's attacks, you need to look at your life and get very honest with yourself. First Peter 5:8 says we must "be sober, be vigilant." In other words, pay attention. Take stock. Make sure you're not doing anything that is leaving the door opened for the devil. If you are, pray and ask God to forgive you. He always will.

First John 1:9 tells us, "If we confess our sins, he is faithful and just and will forgive us our sins and purify us from all unrighteousness" (NIV). When we confess our sins to God and ask for forgiveness, He is faithful to forgive us and to take that sin away. Then we will have locked the doors and windows, and set the alarm on Satan, and he will no longer have an easy way to get in and steal from us.

So if you want to devil-proof your family, first ask yourself if there is any sin in your life. If so, get rid of it. That's like turning on God's security system. Then you can have the assurance that the enemy won't be able to just waltz in and take whatever he wants from you.

Paradise lost

The first human sin is what opened the door to the enemy that day in the garden. Adam and Eve rebelled against God. She ate. He ate. And paradise was lost, not only for them and their children but also for every person who would ever be born. Their sin produced a curse on the earth that continues to this day. The pain, misery, and death of that curse is borne by every human being.

Every marriage has to come face-to-face with the effects of this curse at some time. This was our marriage story. The curse was about to destroy us. The sin in our lives was taking a heavy toll, but Trudi cried out to God one night and Jesus Christ changed her life. She met the Lord and was born again. Her life was radically transformed.

She told me all about her conversion. Of course, she wanted me to follow God too, but I was resisting. She knew she couldn't talk me into getting saved, so she was very sneaky. She prayed for me. I didn't know she was doing that, but I began to feel conflicted—big time.

We didn't use that term in the seventies, but looking back,

walked in the door and I immediately knew she had been crying. I could see it in her eyes.

But I also saw something else in those eyes that I couldn't understand. There was a tangible joy and peace all over her as she breathlessly began to share the details of the day.

"Well, you know the argument we had last night," she began.

I well knew about that argument. Arguments were becoming a regular part of our married life. We had fought about something, and she had gotten so upset that she stormed out of our little apartment and didn't come back for hours.

"I was so upset," she continued, "that I prayed. I told God I needed some help. I told Him I thought marrying you would make me happy but that all we do anymore is fight."

That stung but I had to admit it was true. She said she told God, "I have gone to church all my life (Trudi's dad was an elder in a denominational church in our town, and growing up she was at church every time the doors opened), and as far as I can tell I have never seen You do *anything* for me in my life."

"Whoa," I remember thinking, "that's pretty bold if you're talking to God."

"I told God I had to have some help. I needed to know He really existed. I told Him if He didn't do something to show me He was real, that's it. I would never go to church again as long as I lived. And I really meant it! And today God answered me! It took Him less than twenty-four hours!

Her sister and brother-in-law stopped by and told her how they had really met Jesus just a few weeks earlier. They explained the joy and peace that had come into their lives after they had eceived Him and how they had also experienced something alled the baptism of the Holy Spirit.

She told them they were the answer to her prayer and that wanted what they had. "Kenny," she said, looking me in the "this afternoon I got saved and filled with the Spirit."

"conflicted" would best describe the emotional turmoil I was experiencing as I drove down a vast expanse of farmland to Market Road on a hot July day in 1971.

The plains of the west Texas panhandle where I grew up are a very unique part of this country. The flat landscape, plus the absence of trees (somebody said the only trees we have there are telephone poles, and that is not far from the truth) allows you to literally see for miles. I am still amazed at how flat it is when I go back to visit now. But the desolation and vastness of the landscape is also the setting for the most beautiful sunsets you'll find in America.

The population there is very sparse, and there are no big cities to block your view. I was raised in a farming town that boasted eight hundred people, but I think they must have counted anything that moved. My 1969 graduating class had thirty-five students in it.

In July 1971 I had been married for just a few months to my seventeen-year-old high school sweetheart, Trudi Burk, after spending just one year in college. I was still attempting to go to school part time, play drums in a rock band part time (it was the era of garage bands; everybody wanted to be the Beatles), and hold down a part-time job to try to make ends meet. But at the ripe ol
age of twenty, I was feeling like a full-time failure.

I was now drinking on a daily basis. I didn't want to ad
but I was on the road to alcoholism. And that was the r
was driving down that desolate road that day. You see
County, where we lived, was a dry county, so you h
thirty miles to the next county to buy liquor.

And now another quandary had been added

It had only been a few weeks since I had
work and school, expecting to spend a
dinner and a six-pack, and Trudi had dro

That had been five weeks earlier. The change in her life was palpable and nothing short of amazing. She was like a different person. She was kinder and sweeter than ever before. And she was always reading the Bible, like she really liked it! But more than anything, I had witnessed a peace and contentment on her like I had never seen on anybody in my life. I had to admit that something really had happened to her.

She talked to me about serving God, but I kept giving her the excuse that I was not ready yet. Truthfully, my mom took me to church when I was young. I had even professed to believe in Christ when I was eleven years old, but I had gotten totally away from God. I had turned my back on the one I had given my life to as a child, and the guilt of that weighed heavily on me.

"Surely God doesn't want me anymore," I thought. "Besides, Trudi is just a better person than me. She doesn't have all the issues I am dealing with. There is no way Jesus can love me in my condition of sin."

I wanted to get away to think. My wife's new religious state was driving me crazy, and I wanted something to drink. There was an all-out war going on inside me as I drove down that long, flat highway with all those thoughts bombarding me.

The thing I didn't realize was that Trudi had been praying for me. When I was asleep at night (one of the reasons I drank was because it helped me sleep) she would put her hands on my back and pray for me. Her prayers opened up the door for Jesus to work on my heart.

As I was driving that day, I suddenly sensed someone with me. I know now it was the presence of the Holy Spirit filling my car. And I heard these words, not with my ears but with my heart, "I am the Lord. I am Jesus. I love you." I could never describe how powerful this moment was. The only way I know how to describe it is to say it seemed to melt my heart.

God Almighty was speaking to me. The words continued, "I love you. I want to help you. Why don't you ask Me to help you?"

God knew exactly what I needed. See, I thought I was too far gone to come back to God. I had professed my faith in Christ when I was a kid but had totally walked away from Him. Because of that, I didn't think Jesus could love me anymore. I thought I had committed the unpardonable sin (Satan uses that line on a lot of folks).

But Jesus reached out to me with His love. He loved me in the middle of my mess. He said, "I love you. I want to help you." The Bible says the same thing.

> But God demonstrates His own love toward us, in that while we were still sinners, Christ died for us.
>
> —ROMANS 5:8

God didn't reach out to condemn or put me down. He didn't tell me how dirty I was because of the sins I had committed (and let me tell you, they were many). He didn't tell me, "If you'll change then maybe I can do something with you." No. He reached out to me in love. And I could tell this love accepted me just like I was.

Jesus will never come to condemn you because of your sin. He wants to come into a person's heart first, and then He will give him the grace to change his ways.

Walking with God is always a two-way street. There is a part that only God can do, and there is a part only *we* can do. It is a partnership.

God did His part first. We did not deserve it, but Jesus was nailed to a cross to pay for the mess we all made. Because of that it really doesn't matter how muddled up your marriage may seem to be or how far your children are away from God. Our part is to accept that sacrifice, ask God to forgive our sins, and receive His forgiveness.

Jesus's death on the cross was the most amazing act of love in the universe. And He did it not simply because He loves us—but because He *is* love. But love must be acted on to be activated. In my car that day, Jesus told me, "I love you." But He also said, "Why don't you *ask* Me to help you?"

God's love is there for everyone. Jesus died for the entire world. God's will was and is for every person to be saved and know Him. God didn't come to this earth to judge you. He came to forgive and then empower you to change. He did His part. The question is, will you do yours? The only way you can devil-proof your family is if your life is built on the firm foundation of Jesus Christ.

I will never forget that encounter with God back in 1971. I didn't do it right then while I was driving, but a few days later I did ask Jesus to help me. His power and presence flooded my heart. I committed my life to Him. I really meant business with God, and there was an immediate change. He saved me and then filled me with the power of the Holy Spirit.

Rebuilding the hedge

In the garden Adam and Eve lost their love connection with God because of their disobedience. And when their relationship with God was severed, everything changed. Their authority became skewed because they had allowed the devil to enter.

When the hedge came down that day in the Garden of Eden it opened the door for every vile and wicked design of Satan to enter. The curse entered the earth, and every person who would ever be born would have to bear its consequences. The result of Adam and Eve's sin was a crippled marriage and dysfunction among their children. (Cain killed his brother Abel; that's sibling rivalry on steroids!) But the major thing it did was separate mankind from the Father who loved them.

But Jesus came. If we're not careful, we can hear that so many times we stop thinking about what it really means. God came to this earth as a human! *Wow.* Let the miraculous truth of that wash over you. Think about it. God came for you and me. We are the reason He came. He wanted to rescue us from the trap we had fallen into.

Jesus is called the second Adam. He represents the alternate plan. Jesus came to rebuild the breach in the hedge. He defeated the devil on the cross so our hearts could be united to the Father once again. He restored the authority Adam lost so the gap in the hedge could be closed.

But the devil didn't die. He is alive and well on planet Earth. There is still a curse in place that he vigorously enforces. It is only through our cooperation with Jesus and the Holy Spirit that we can walk victoriously over this curse. So it is our job to serve the devil an eviction notice and enforce it with our faith. Simply put, through Christ you can kick the devil out of your house!

Maybe you are facing severe marriage problems as you read this today. Maybe your kids are a mess. Jesus can help you. He can restore the joy in your marriage and empower you to set a godly example for your children. I speak from experience. He did it for me, and I know He can do it for you. That is why I have dedicated my life to preaching this message called the gospel. Jesus came to empower you to not only go to heaven when you die, but His grace is powerful and practical enough to fix any and all family challenges.

Through Jesus Christ you have been given what it takes to repair the breach in your personal family hedge. Whatever family issue you face today, Jesus is the great healer of pain, and the application of His Word can restore your hedge and recover what the enemy has stolen. But how does that look? Keep reading. That's what we are going to find out.

PART II

DEVIL-PROOF YOUR MARRIAGE

Chapter 2

GOD'S DESIGN FOR MARRIAGE

I'LL NEVER FORGET the first time I saw Trudi. I was in the ninth grade. Because I grew up on a farm, I got my driver's license when I was fourteen, which was allowed in our county because young teenagers like myself were often needed to drive the farm equipment. After I got my license, my dad was nice enough to buy me my own car. It was a 1963 four-door Ford Galaxy 500 with a 390 V-8 engine—and it was huge. This car was so big I could have leased out the backseat to somebody as an apartment to live in.

The irony of me having such a big car was that I was so little. At fourteen I stood at about five-foot-three and weighed 140 pounds soaking wet. In order for me to see to drive this monster I had to look between the gap of the steering wheel and the dashboard. I was so short, when people saw my car tooling around town it looked like nobody was driving it!

So there I was sitting in my car, listening to the radio with one of my friends as we watched kids board the bus for a school trip to a spring choir competition. In a lot of schools it wasn't cool to be in the choir, but our school had an award-winning choir, so all the cool kids were in choir. And, of course, I was one of the coolest.

As I glanced over to look at the kids getting on the bus, I saw what appeared to be an angel from heaven! She was blonde and was wearing yellow shorts and a yellow top. I had never seen this girl before and I could only see her from the back, but I really liked what I saw from the back! I turned to my friend and said, "Who is that girl? I've never seen her before."

He told me, "That's Brad Burk's sister, Trudi. She's in the seventh grade." Even though our school was very small (only thirty-five people in my graduating class) I had never seen her because our classes were in different buildings. I was in high school, and she was in junior high.

I made a mental note: "Sometime today see what that girl looks like from the front." I did see her from the front later that day, and even though she was only twelve, I liked what I saw equally as well as, if not better than, the back.

This is the girl who would become my girlfriend off and on all during high school. This is the girl I would end up marrying, and the future mother of my children and grandmother of our grandchildren. This is the girl I've been married to for forty-four years.

But our relationship didn't begin because I was spiritually drawn to her. I was not attracted to her because of the way her mind worked. I knew nothing about either of those things the first time I laid eyes on her. That would come later. My first attraction to Trudi was totally physical.

This is the way attraction between men and women usually works. We first notice each other physically. If there is an interest there, then we get to know each other mentally and discover each other's personalities. If there is a connection and it is so strong we want to make a deep commitment, the next step is the big one. That's when we decide we want to be life partners. It is called marriage. Ideally this is the way attraction to the opposite sex should work.

Marriage is two people making a life commitment to join in what is known in the Bible as covenant. Covenant is the strongest agreement that can be made between two people. They publicly vow before God and each other to be partners for the rest of their lives. That's how the Bible tells us marriage is designed to work—it is supposed to last our entire time on the earth or until one partner passes away.

When it comes to human relationships, there is none higher than marriage. You may have a good friend in life, or you may dearly love your mama, but there is no relationship on the earth that causes you to become one with another human being like you are in marriage. The only other relationship like it is when we become Christians; the Bible says we then become one with Christ. (See 1 Corinthians 6:17.)

Marriage is the complete joining of two people in every part of their being—body, soul, and spirit. When a couple makes their wedding vows in the presence of God, a blessing comes on them, and they are made one spiritually. In the eyes of God they are linked together. They physically become one when they consummate their union, but the joining of a man and woman in marriage goes so deep we will never totally understand the depth of its meaning. The Bible calls it a mystery.

> As the Scriptures say, "A man leaves his father and mother and is joined to his wife, and the two are united into one." This is a great mystery, but it is an illustration of the way Christ and the church are one.
>
> —Ephesians 5:31–32, NLT

The joining together of a couple on a mental, or soul, level requires that they learn how each other thinks and honor the differences they have as individuals and as men and women. This doesn't come naturally, and not understanding how their spouse thinks is a major reason many marriages disintegrate into divorce. It is an area of uniting that couples must constantly work on.

I have been married to Trudi for forty-four years. You would think after that long I would have her totally figured out. But not so! She still surprises me. I continue to peel off layers of learning about this beautiful female creature called Trudi. Even after all these years I have to continue to work on my ability to communicate effectively with her.

Because of the holiness and importance of the marriage relationship, it is the number one relationship the devil attacks. And he is having a great deal of success when you look at just a few of the statistics concerning the state of marriage in the United States.

The divorce rate is nearly double what it was in 1960.[1]

Sixty percent of those who get married between the ages of twenty and twenty-five end up in divorce.[2]

Fifty percent of marriages in which the bride is over twenty-five end in divorce.[3]

Sixty-five percent of people who live together get married. But people who live together before marriage are more likely to get divorced.[4]

Studies indicate that daughters of divorced parents have a 65 percent higher divorce rate in marriage than children of non-divorced parents, and sons have a 35 percent higher divorce rate.[5]

We will go into much detail about how men and women think later and share insights that will help couples grow together, but for now understand this: the key to making a marriage better is being willing to learn what your spouse needs and grow and change together with the help of the Holy Spirit.

God made us one-of-a-kind

God created the man first in the Garden of Eden. Have you ever thought about why God chose to do it that way? He could have made the man and the woman at the same time. In fact, God could have created a hundred people, or a million. We're told there are more than seven billion people living on the earth right now. God could have created all seven billion at one time. After all, He is God.

But He created only one person. Why is that? I believe in this for many reasons. First of all, God was stamping on creation the importance of the individual. Every person is uniquely made. Of all those seven billion people living on the planet right now (notwithstanding those who have lived and died since the creation of the earth six thousand years ago), no two people are the same.

Have you ever been told you looked like somebody else? I have been told on more than one occasion that I look like the actor James Caan. I guess maybe I do look like him, because I've been told that a number of times. I've also been told more than once that I sound like Johnny Cash, which I think is pretty cool.

But I am not those people. I am myself, and out of all the people in the earth there is nobody exactly like me. And there is nobody just like you, either. My point is this: every person originated with God in heaven, and we were all sent here for a unique and wonderful purpose. Every person is original.

Let the beauty of what these verses say about God's creation sink into your heart:

> Thank you for making me so wonderfully complex! Your workmanship is marvelous—how well I know it. You watched me as I was being formed in utter seclusion, as I was woven together in the dark of the womb.
>
> —Psalm 139:14–15, NLT

> Your eyes saw me unformed, yet in Your book all my days were written, before any of them came into being. How precious also are Your thoughts to me, O God! How great is the sum of them!
>
> —Psalm 139:16–17, MEV

These verses describe the intricacy and detail with which God made every person. Before we even got here to the earth, God recorded our lives in a book. Let me tell you something that you should let blow your mind on a daily basis: God made you just the way you are and He loves you much more than you will ever know or your mind can possibly comprehend. I pray you never forget that. To me, that is truly so *awesome*.

Your hands are one of the things that identifies your originality. You have tiny grooves in your fingertips called fingerprints that are different from all the other seven billion people on earth. No two people have the same fingerprints. With a retina scan, you can be identified by your eyes, because no two people have the same eyes. You also have a voice print that identifies you. No two people have the exact same voice print. How did God do that? Let's just say He's very good at what He does!

Now consider this. Psychologists have discovered that when you have a thought or an idea, it instantly moves through seven channels, or seven tracks, in your brain. These seven areas of the brain were revealed through imaging techniques that observe people's brain activity as they perform certain tasks. God knew about this even before our modern-day geniuses.[6] The Bible actually speaks about this:

> Wisdom has built her house, she has hewn out her seven pillars.
>
> —PROVERBS 9:1, MEV

God Himself created your brain with seven pillars. Every person's thoughts move through these seven different tracks, but it has been scientifically proven that no two people's thought patterns are exactly the same. Even the way you think and process information is totally unique to anyone else ever created. This is amazing! The saying "When God made you He broke the mold" is very valid and true. There is no one quite like you; you were created just the way you are by an amazing God who loves you.

Maybe you were born out of wedlock and you think sometimes that you shouldn't even be here. Maybe your parents have drilled into your brain that you are not as good as your brothers or sisters. Maybe you were sexually abused by someone in your family and you face extreme self-loathing and hate your very existence. You may feel like you are just a mistake.

Listen to me. Those are lies from the pit of hell. No matter what you've been through and how you may feel about yourself, God made you and loves you—just the way you are. No matter what hurt and disappointment you may have experienced, no matter how much devastation sin has caused in your life—God has a great purpose for your existence.

Another reason God made Adam first was to establish the man as the leader of the marriage. I didn't say man was the boss and was created first so he could order his wife around. That is not the way this is supposed to work. Marriage is a partnership.

A marriage partnership

Genesis 2:7 powerfully reveals how God designed the marriage partnership to work:

> Then the LORD God formed man from the dust of the ground and breathed into his nostrils the breath of life, and man became a living being.
>
> —MEV

The word translated *man* in this passage is the Hebrew word *adam*. It actually comes from a root word that means ruddy or red.[7] Another way to describe this is to say man, or Adam, actually means "blood man." Adam was created in the image of God but he had blood. Humans must have blood that flows through our veins in order to live. The life of flesh is in our blood (Lev. 17:11). No blood equals no more life.

From the time Adam is created through these next few verses of Genesis 2 the word for man is the same. But after the woman is created from the man, the word for man changes.

> Then the rib which the LORD God had taken from man, He made into a woman, and He brought her to the man. Then Adam said, "This is now bone of my bones and flesh of my flesh; she will be called Woman, for she was taken out of Man.
>
> —GENESIS 2:22–23, MEV

The Hebrew word for *man* stays the same all the way through Genesis 2 including verse 22. But in verse 23 a totally different Hebrew word is used. In the English it is still translated "man," but instead of *adam* the word *iysh* is used. The word *iysh* actually means "fire." The word translated *woman* also changes in verse 23 to *'iyshshah,* which means "came from fire."[8]

Why did the word for man change? Notice what happens in verse 23. The woman has been taken from the man. Adam had surgery that day in the garden. Maybe Adam was coming out of the anesthesia when he saw her for the first time. Adam had seen every plant and animal God created and even gave them names. But he had never seen anything like this beautiful creature, and he was blown away by what he saw.

When he laid his eyes on the woman that day some kind of change happened within him. We can tell by the declaration he made when he saw her:

> And Adam said: "This is now bone of my bones and flesh of my flesh; she shall be called Woman, because she was taken out of Man." Therefore a man shall leave

> his father and mother and be joined to his wife, and
> they shall become one flesh.
>
> —Genesis 2:23–24

This was, in essence, Adam's revelation about the woman. He says she will be "flesh of my flesh." This is a recognition of the physical attraction and passion that was birthed in him when the woman came on the scene. The statement that she will be "bone of my bones" is a recognition of the inner strength the woman would supply to the marriage. Bones represent structure. Without bones your body would just be a heap of flesh. Adam is recognizing that the woman would be a partner who would strengthen him so together they could fulfill the unique purpose they had been created for.

This word *iysh,* or fire, refers to a new spark of life, a new passion both physically and spiritually that was born in Adam when he looked upon this woman for the first time. This included a physical attraction like I experienced when I saw Trudi for the very first time, but it goes much deeper than that. This is speaking of a brand-new purpose and vision for life that Adam never had until the day he met and married this amazing woman.

This fire also represents a new anointing or supernatural empowerment from heaven that came on both of them that day. The very presence of God Himself united Adam and Eve, and it came to empower them for this brand-new union God was creating that day. Their marriage was a holy thing.

Marriage is designed to be blessed by God. It was conceived by God to take two unique individuals to a new level of life with each other and to a new and more powerful dimension with God.

When Adam and Eve met, it was love at first sight. Adam names her "woman." He was saying, "This creature is different.

She came from me. She is my life partner, and now together we will accomplish something I could have never done alone."

He says the woman is "bone of my bone." I believe that statement goes even deeper than her physical creation.

Think about how your bones work. Bones are the physical strength of your body. Bones are the core that gives your body structure. Without bones you would just be a pile of flesh. But your bones give you physical stability needed to move and live.

Adam recognized this woman would provide him a hidden strength he didn't have alone. Why hidden? Many times the wife is the one who gives advice behind the scenes to provide the husband with wisdom he couldn't see without her. God must have given Adam a revelation of those truths the first time he saw Eve.

He saw that she would bring the wisdom and counsel he would need to fulfill his purpose. He must have seen that this new bride was about to take him to a new level of life that he could never achieve alone.

The fire of God

God brought Eve to Adam. He presented Adam with his bride. You could call this an arranged marriage orchestrated by a loving Father. Although it is not described in the first few chapters of Genesis, a wedding took place that day in the Garden of Eden. Eve was created and then immediately presented to her bridegroom, covered by the glory of God. Eve didn't have to wear white, because she was covered by the purity of the glory of God.

Adam and Eve were married that day in the garden with the new names *iysh* ("fire") and *iyshshah* ("came from fire"). Think with me about how fire works. When fire is under control it is a great blessing. I love the fireplace in my house. A crackling fire is a source of heat in the winter and relaxing to watch. But if the fire jumped out of the fireplace and spilled onto the floor of my living room, my attitude would quickly change. The fire that blesses me when it is controlled could also burn my house down if it were allowed to escape. Uncontrolled fire produces destruction.

Another form of fire is electricity. I love electricity. Without it there would be no air-conditioning in the summer. My computer and phone couldn't be charged, and I wouldn't be writing this book on my iPad right now. Electricity is one of the most essential ingredients we must have to live fully in our time. If you don't believe me, remember how it feels when you lose power because of a storm. Everything changes without electrical power.

But electricity can also kill you. When it is not kept under control through good wiring and proper connections, it can be the source of great pain and even death.

You and your spouse were created with fire in your being. Why do you have such heated arguments in your marriage? Some of the reason is the passion that exists between the two of you. When you don't know how to handle your emotions, this fire seeks to destroy you. The passion that brings two people together in marriage is the same passion that can destroy marriages through strife. But don't worry. This book will teach you some new skills to manage that passion.

Remember, part of this fire between a husband and wife is actually the presence of God Himself. Marriage is not designed to be just two people. At its best marriage is the union of three: a man, a woman, and God. Marriage will never reach its highest potential unless Jesus and His presence are with you.

Remember when Adam and Eve ate the forbidden fruit that day?

> At that moment their eyes were opened, and they suddenly felt shame at their nakedness. So they sewed fig leaves together to cover themselves.
>
> —Genesis 3:7, nlt

What an awful moment! When the first couple willfully disobeyed God that fateful day, they saw the change that instantly took place. They felt shame at what they had done. They now saw that they were naked and exposed. They desperately tried to cover up, but they couldn't seem to cover their guilt and shame.

When they sinned against God, they removed the cover He had set in place and opened the door for every vile and wicked sin to legally enter planet Earth. A curse was unleashed on humanity. This is why we have sickness, disease, poverty, despair, and every wicked imagination that can be conceived, ultimately producing death. Because of their sin that day, the door was opened wide for Satan to enter in with all his wicked schemes.

Adam and Eve lost their access to the glory and presence of God. Their sin separated them from the Father they had walked with, and they literally died on the inside, in their spirits. The covering that had protected them from being naked was actually God Himself. But when they opened the door to sin, they could no longer be in God's presence, because God is holy and cannot dwell in the presence of sin.

Remember when God came looking for Adam and Eve after they sinned? The Bible says, "Then the Lord God called to the man, 'Where are you?'" (Gen. 3:9, nlt). God was not physically looking for Adam and Eve. He knew where they were because no one can hide from God. What He was really asking was, "Where is the light?"[9]

The light, the fire of God, was gone. His presence had departed. What a sad day. God was confronting them with the truth by asking them where they were. He was also asking, "Where are you with Me?" This was a father who was confronting His children who had done wrong—He wanted them to confess and tell Him the truth.

It's like a parent who catches his children disobeying and asks them, "What are you doing?" He knows what they are doing. He can see it. He is looking for them to admit it and show remorse.

Adam and Eve tried to cover themselves and their tracks. They used fig leaves. Eve tried to blame the serpent. Adam tried to blame his wife (this is what happens many times in marriage; we try to cast blame for our problems on each other). And in the height of arrogance, he tried to blame God!

> The man replied, "It was the woman you [God] gave me..."
>
> —Genesis 3:12, nlt

Since that time man has sought ways to cover the guilt and darkness that every person experiences, to no avail. Sadly, man cannot cover himself—no way, no how. But God in His love and compassion prepared a covering for them.

> And the Lord God made clothing from animal skins for Adam and his wife.
>
> —Genesis 3:21, nlt

Despite all the harm and pain Adam and Eve had caused, God made them clothing and dressed them. Remarkably, the Hebrew word for skins here is *owr* (or *ohr*), which is also a homonym that means "light."[10]

When God dressed them in *owr*, He was telling them that all was not lost. Yes, their sin had put out the light and snuffed out the fire of God's presence. But in clothing them with animal skins, God was literally prophesying that a new day would come when the light would come back and be revealed. He was prophesying the coming Messiah, Jesus—the return of the light!

That is exactly why Jesus came. He doesn't just put a cover over our sin; His blood cleanses and does away with our sin—our sin is wiped out when we choose to believe He died on the cross. The Bible says, "He canceled the record of the charges against us and took it away by nailing it to the cross" (Col. 2:14, NLT). When we accept Christ as our Savior, our sin is removed, and the presence of God, the fire that left Adam and Eve, is restored to us. God moves in with His very presence to now help us in our human weakness and frailty.

Handle with care

It is the fire of God's presence that joins marriages together, but it must be handled properly. There was a man named Uzzah in the Bible who mishandled God's presence, and it cost him his life (2 Sam. 6). God's presence is serious business.

God designed marriage to be an intensely impassioned and spirited union. The passion that brings a couple together as husband and wife was designed to empower them and take them to levels of life they could never achieve alone. But if we don't understand how God designed this fire to work, the devil will work overtime to ignite things that shouldn't be lit.

God gave us this gift of fire to bless marriages and empower couples to fulfill their unique purpose and vision. But we have to learn how to control this passion through our obedience to God's Word.

I mentioned earlier that Trudi and I got married young. The physical passion was there, but we didn't understand how marriage was designed to work. Before we learned some things, we had many combustible moments that threatened to burn our house down, even after we were saved and knew Jesus.

See, great marriages don't just happen. Whether your marriage makes it or not is not just the luck of the draw. Successful marriages are built. If you want your marriage to last, you must be willing to get outside your comfort zone to better understand your spouse, but the work is worth it. If you are facing some intense fire that threatens to destroy your marriage, the things you will learn in this book can change your marriage forever—*if* you will apply them.

Notice what else Adam said the day he met Eve for the first time:

> Therefore shall a man leave his father and his mother, and shall cleave unto his wife: and they shall be one flesh.
>
> —Genesis 2:24, kjv

The word *cleave* in the original Hebrew is very revealing when it comes to making this fire, or passion, in your marriage work. Cleave here means to cling to, pursue, or chase. Most couples spend time dating or courting before making a marriage commitment. This is a time when we are on the hunt for each other. When we are in pursuit, we put our best foot forward. We are trying to win our future spouse, so we make everything extra special.

When I was dating Trudi, I would spend time cleaning up my car. I would carefully shower, put on cologne, and comb my hair. I would brush my teeth and always have a mint with me because I wanted my breath to be just right. I would make sure I was on time, and if I was running behind I would call her and explain why I was late.

When we court someone we usually try to project the best image because we are in pursuit. But once we win the person, if we are not careful we stop chasing. We allow the romance to leave and everything becomes common and mundane. The Bible says we are to "cleave." According to this scripture, we should never stop pursuing and chasing each other, even if we've been married forty-four years.

Another illustration that can be used to explain the meaning of the word cleave is to be welded together. Welding is when two individual pieces of metal are heated to the point of melting and then are joined together. White-hot heat is used for the positive to unite two separated pieces into one.

Welding illustrates how God designed marriage to work. If a weld is done successfully, the joint where the two pieces of metal meet can sustain more stress than any other part of the metal. This is the way God wants your marriage to be. Stress will come. The devil will initiate attacks against you. The troubles of life will try to pull you apart. But when you cleave to each other and keep your weld strong, you will have the strength to repel those attacks.

Marriage is designed to join two people who with their individual, unique abilities will be able to defeat the invasions that attack their union—if they will work together. The key is that we never stop cleaving and working on our marriage connection. As we keep pursuing each other we develop a house so strong that all the stresses of life the enemy throws at us can be overcome.

> Two people are better off than one, for they can help each other succeed.
>
> —ECCLESIASTES 4:9, NLT

You are better together than apart. God designed your union to take you to a higher level of success together than you could reach on your own. But establishing this in your marriage is not automatic. You must be willing to put in some time and make an investment. In the next several chapters we are going to show you spiritual and practical ways you can make investments in your marriage that will yield dividends for your future. I promise it is well worth it.

I love my children and I enjoy my career calling to preach God's Word. But the most precious thing I have is my marriage to Trudi. Our commitment to each other is the core that makes everything else work.

So to recap, God designed your marriage to be a partnership. He gave you a passion that is meant to take you to higher levels as a couple than you could reach on your own. But you must handle this fire with care. Take the time to pursue your spouse; keep learning what he or she likes and desires. This will help your marriage become strong enough to handle life's storms and repel the devil's attacks.

Chapter 3

THE KEY TO A HAPPY, LOVING MARRIAGE

WHEN YOU BOIL it down, there are three basic areas the enemy tries to use to cause division in your marriage: communication, intimacy, and finances. In this chapter we will focus on communication because it typically triggers the problems in the other two areas. Intimacy issues can be solved if there are open lines of communication and couples are willing to talk about the problems they are having. Money issues are the same. You could say good communication is *the* key to a happy, loving, lasting marriage.

But the challenge is that men and women communicate very differently, and that is by design. To understand why God created men and women with such different communication styles, we must again look to the Garden of Eden.

> And the LORD God formed man of the dust of the ground, and breathed into his nostrils the breath of life; and man became a living being.
>
> —GENESIS 2:7

Adam was created from the dust of the ground; he came from dirt. When you think about men, they often like that dirt. Many men like to go outside; they like to hunt, fish, ride four-wheelers, play golf. It's not that women don't enjoy these things, but men don't seem to mind getting dirty as much as women do.

Of course, I'm generalizing here. You may be able to think of couples who don't fit this mold—perhaps you and your spouse don't fit this paradigm. But it often works this way for men and women. Dirt seems to call to men, possibly because they were formed from the dirt. Women, on the other hand, didn't come from dirt (men, that's why they don't like us bringing our dirt into the house). Eve came from man.

Here is an example of what I mean. One of my favorite outdoor activities is to go to the beach. I know some people love the warm water of the Gulf Coast or the beaches in Florida, but personally I love the beaches of Southern California. When Trudi and I preach in churches out there I normally schedule an extra day or two to spend at the beach.

The water of the Pacific Ocean is colder than the southern waters of the Atlantic, but that doesn't bother me. The cooler water is invigorating.

My favorite beach is Laguna. I'll jump into the cold water and let the waves roll over me. The swells usually come in patterns. There will be six to ten waves, fairly consistent in size, then a wave will come that is so big and powerful it can knock you down.

I've had some waves slam me around so hard I've been bruised and physically battered. One time a wave jammed my head into the sand, taking the top layer of skin off my forehead. It hit me so hard that I was dazed as I came out of the water and walked out on the beach.

But I still love the beach. I love the vastness of the ocean, the smell of salt in the air. I don't mind getting sand all over me—in my ears and between my toes. I just love the whole beach experience.

Trudi likes to go to the beach with me, but she has a different way of enjoying it. She likes listening to the waves crash, smelling the sea air, and pondering the vastness of the ocean. The beach is one of her favorite places to pray.

But when she goes to the beach, she likes to sit in a beach chair with a cup of coffee. She doesn't like to get too close to the water. She parks her chair a good distance from the waves so there is no danger of a rogue wave reaching her. She will walk down the beach with me and maybe get her feet wet, but that's as far as it goes. She has absolutely no interest in riding waves. In fact, the thought of getting ocean water in her hair is repulsive to her.

This goes back to creation. God put differences in men and women from the beginning, and we need to honor these differences if we are going to communicate successfully.

Trudi and I travel to many churches across the United States and around the world teaching family principles from the Bible, and these differences in men and women seem to be true everywhere we go. We have ministered in meetings specifically for men and in meetings specifically for women, and we've found that if those events are to be successful they must be structured very differently.

A man's meeting must have elements that appeal to men. The location is important. The last one we hosted was in Raton, New Mexico, in the foothills of the Rocky Mountains. We called it "Be the Man," and it was held at the Whittington Center, one of the nation's premiere gun ranges.

The meeting lasted two days. I corralled a band of excellent musicians, and the praise and worship times were exceptional. We chose songs that would appeal to men, songs that spoke of conquering and victory. When we got into worship, I was blessed to hear men's voices singing loudly as they worshipped the King. I've heard it said that men don't like to worship, but I don't buy that. Men were made to worship Jesus. They just need to be allowed to worship in a way that appeals to them.

The meeting room was nothing fancy. In fact, it was like a metal barn with a concrete floor. The event was held in May, and the weather in New Mexico is usually warm that time of year. But that year, a freak snowstorm hit just north of our location the week of our event. We didn't have snow, but the temperature dropped to 17 degrees one night.

We had no heat in the building, so it was really cold. But those guys put on their camouflage deer hunting gear, and not one man bailed out of our services. I challenged the men by saying, "It's cold, guys. But we are men and a little cold won't stop us, right?" They answered with a loud, "*Nooo!*" Tough conditions caused them to rally for the cause. I didn't hear one man complain about the temperature the entire meeting. When those men were challenged, they rose to the occasion.

Those men sang and worshipped God. They were very attentive to the Word of God that was preached. The speakers dealt with hard-hitting subjects like pornography, childhood wounds, and how to treat your wife. We had powerful altar calls, and the presence of God was strong. But we didn't have services nonstop. We gave the men time to enjoy outdoor activities. Men brought their guns and we shot trap, skeet, and many varied targets at the world-class gun range. We also fished in the mountains and held a golf tournament. We had a lot of fun.

We concluded the meeting with a meal we called "All the Meat You Can Eat." We grilled steaks, burgers, brisket, sausages, hot dogs, and more, with sides of every description. If it was beef, we ate it. And those men stuffed themselves until they could barely move.

That meeting worked for men. But it wouldn't have appealed to many women. Trudi has ministered in many ladies' meetings, and there are certain elements that have made them successful. The events are usually held in a nice venue, either the church auditorium or at a hotel. The room is normally lavishly decorated, and the women tend to dress up, even when the tone of the event is causal. You'll see heels and fancy purses, but not a lot of camouflage.

In my experience women have more services and workshops than men do, and they last longer. They will start early in the morning and have services into the evening. After the services, they have prayer time that is normally filled with a lot of crying and hugging. I don't say this to disparage women. In fact, women seem to be much more spiritually open than men. They seem to be more inclined than men are to wait upon the Lord and move with Him. I say this only to note the God-given differences between men and women.

Women eat differently too. There normally is not as much beef on the menu. Women will eat little sandwiches with the crust cut off. They eat quiche. They like to eat petit fours (Trudi had to tell me what those were), salads, and vegetables that they can dip into ranch dressing or hummus. We have brisket at our men's meetings, not broccoli.

Groups of men and groups of women communicate differently too. Let's say you have a table with six men sitting around it. The conversation around the table is very orderly. When men communicate, they take turns talking. One man will speak, and everyone else will listen. When he is done speaking, someone else will pick up the conversation with his comments.

But women don't do that. If there are six women at a table, you will probably see multiple conversations going on at once. In fact, sometimes all six women will be talking—at the same time! It sounds like mass confusion to a man, but my wife tells me (I didn't pick this up on my own; she had to explain it to me) that although they are all talking, they can hear what each woman is saying and understand it all. That is very confusing to the average man.

A strong military ally

This all goes back to Adam in the garden. Let's look again at Genesis 2.

After God created the man, He planted a garden and placed Adam there (Gen. 2:8). God gave Adam a home. Then the Bible says He gave the man a job, which was to tend the garden (Gen. 2:15). God did this because men need to accomplish something. In the beginning, God gave man a sense of purpose and gave him a vision to accomplish that purpose.

So there is Adam, living in a wonderful paradise. Perfect weather. No weeds to fight or storms to fear. His life on the farm must have been easy and very fulfilling. Adam had been given a vision for life, and he was walking in his purpose.

On top of all that, he was walking in close fellowship with God. He was enjoying all the animals God had created and partnered with God to name them all. Adam's life was good. He could sit in his recliner when he wanted to, put his feet up even if they were dirty, and take total control of the remote. But God stepped back from this situation and made a startling comment:

> And the LORD God said, It is not good that the man should be alone; I will make him an help meet for him.
>
> —GENESIS 2:18, KJV

For the first time since Creation, God says something is not good. At the end of each of the six days of Creation, God declared that what He made was good. But then in Genesis 2, for the very first time, God declares that something is *not* good. He said it wasn't good for the man to be alone.

Here God was stamping His design and approval on the covenant of marriage, but God was also saying that people were not made to be alone. We need other people in our lives. We were not made to be hermits. Whether married or single, it's not good for anybody to be alone.

Think about how financial blessing comes our way. God knows we need money to live and survive, but He doesn't just rain money down from heaven on us. Finances come through the medium of exchange with other people.

For instance, somebody has a unique gift to cook. He develops that gift and opens a restaurant. People come to the restaurant because they have a need: they are hungry. They are willing to trade a certain amount of money for the quality of food the restaurant provides, and that blesses the person who cooked the food. This exchange blesses both parties.

God designed us to need other people to survive on the planet. Our quality of life is dependent on others. No man or woman was created to be an island.

Because it wasn't good for the man to be alone, God decided to make him "an help meet." Notice that phrase. It does not say God decided to make the man a helpmate. The Darby Translation uses the word "helpmate," but most modern translations use "helper," and the King James Version uses "help meet."

Why am I making such a big deal about this? The word helpmate implies that the woman was made to be Adam's assistant, that she was there to wait on him and follow him around doing his laundry. In many countries around the world this is how women are viewed. Women are treated as second-class citizens. But when you see the intent God had for the creation of woman, you will see that nothing could be further from the truth.

The definition of the word *help meet* reveals to us how God designed marriage to work. This is really critical to understand if you are going to build a long, happy marriage that will withstand the devil's attacks. A marriage secret is revealed once again in the Hebrew language.

The term *help meet* actually comes from two different words.

The Hebrew word for help is *ezer.* There is a book in the Bible called Ezra; that name has *ezer* as its root.[1]

The word translated "meet" is *neged.* This word is very interesting because it is often translated "suitable," but it can also mean "opposite" or even "over against."[2] So put the two words together and they are *ezer neged,* which means a helper opposite, or even a helper against.

Wait a minute. A wife is designed to be a helper against her husband?

The full thought offers a great deal of insight into the kind of helper God was giving Adam. Together the Hebrew letters that make up *ezer neged* create a word picture that actually means "the strong military ally that sees the enemy."[3] Let that sink in.

The woman was created to be strong. Yes, 1 Peter 3:7 calls woman "the weaker vessel," and that may be true physically, but when it comes to mental and spiritual strength, women stand toe to toe with men. God has invested a great inner strength in women.

Men, it is important that we see our spouse as a military ally. Remember, we are in a war. We have an enemy who is serious about our destruction. If you are in a war you need allies. You need people who will stand with you in the fight. One of the reasons couples divorce is that they neglect to see they are on the same team. They buy the enemy's lie that their spouse is their problem. Your spouse is designed to be your ally. You are supposed to be a team working together with common goals.

The wife is not just a military ally, but she "sees the enemy." Women have a God-given ability to see things, both physically and spiritually, that men often don't see. For instance, women see more shades of color than men do. Men see the more primary colors—red, yellow, black, and white—but women see the various shades, such as fuchsia, periwinkle, mauve, aqua, magenta, and lavender.[4] And because women have two X chromosomes, they have the potential to see up to one hundred million colors, where the average male would see about one million.[5]

Men can see farther distances than women, but women seem to have better peripheral vision.[6] God designed it that way, both naturally and spiritually, so that when men and women come together they have better vision.

Men and women process thought differently too. We are speaking generally here, and this doesn't always hold true, but for the most part men think primarily from the left side of the brain, which is the more analytical and logical side of the brain. Women seem to use both sides of the brain, the left and the right, which is the thoughtful, intuitive, and more emotional side.[7]

Women just seem to be wired to take in details that men often miss. Remember when I mentioned that a whole table of women can be talking at the same time? Women can hear more than one conversation at a time. Why did God put that into them? I'm sure God had many reasons for giving women this ability, but it can't hurt for mothers to be able to understand different children when they're talking at the same time.

Often, mothers can tell by a child's cry what he needs. Mothers know their children's mad cry, sad cry, and sick cry. Mothers (and women in general) are great at multitasking. They can be stirring spaghetti and talking on the phone, and still hear what their children in the room are saying.

When we were raising our children, Trudi would pick up on details that I didn't see. One time our son came home from school. He just walked in the door and said hello and then went to his room. Trudi turned to me and said, "Something is wrong with Joshua. He must have had a bad day."

I said, "What do you mean? He seems fine to me."

"No he's not. I can tell something is not right."

"How can you tell?"

"I can tell by his cheeks." She went on to explain that from the time he was a little boy, when he got upset his cheeks would turn red. Even if he tried to hide his feelings, his mama could pick up on it. I had never noticed that until she pointed it out to me.

This is the gift God gave Adam the day He made Eve—a strong military ally, a partner with different gifts than he had. God endowed women with a unique ability to "see the enemy"—to recognize things men don't innately see.

More than just a rib

Let's look at another verse that shows us God's intent for the woman.

> So the LORD God caused the man to fall into a deep sleep. While the man slept, the LORD God took out one of the man's ribs and closed up the opening. Then the LORD God made a woman from the rib, and he brought her to the man.
>
> —GENESIS 2:21–22, NLT

God put Adam under anesthesia and performed surgery while he slept. Remember that the man came from the dust, but the woman was taken from the man. It says here that God took one of his ribs, but this is really not the best translation of the word. It is better stated in the Amplified version.

> And the Lord God caused a deep sleep to fall upon Adam; and while he slept, He took one of his ribs or a part of his side and closed up the [place with] flesh. And the rib or part of his side which the Lord God had taken from the man He built up and made into a woman, and He brought her to the man.
>
> —GENESIS 2:21–22, AMP

Notice it says that God took "part of his side." This is really more in line with the original Hebrew than the English word *rib*. When most people think of a rib, they think about an insignificant little bone. You would never go into a restaurant and say, "I think I'll have a rib." That would be too small. So when people think the woman was made from a rib, they often think she was made from something small—just a rib, something you could take or leave.

Our rib cage is designed to protect our vital organs. It is made up of many different bones on both sides, so if we lost one rib it wouldn't be that big of a deal. But if you lost a whole side, that would be a different story. When God performed surgery on Adam that day, He didn't just remove an insignificant little bone. It is more like He cut Adam in two in order to create the woman. You could live without a rib, but if you lost an entire side of your body you couldn't make it. When God created the woman He was saying, "She is going to be such an important part of your life now, you will not ever be able to exist again properly without her."

Her design was different from Adam's. The Bible says God formed Adam from the dust of the ground. The word "formed" actually means he was molded or squeezed into shape.

But Scripture says God "made" Eve. The Hebrew word translated "made" in Genesis 2:22 also means to be built. The man was squeezed and molded into shape, but God used a much more sophisticated and detailed process to create Eve. She was delicately and intricately—some would even say more complicatedly—designed.

There's another part of the word rib we need to examine. The Hebrew word translated "rib" in Genesis 2:22 is *tselah*. It actually means "for advice."[8] The Jewish sages teach that women were given an extra portion of wisdom that men need. They have a proverb that says, "If a man's wife be short let him bend down and incline his ears to listen to her sage counsel. When in doubt, ask your wife. She was made to give you the best advice."[9]

Adam's bride was created to walk beside him and bring him advice and wisdom so their partnership could produce a higher way of life. Husbands need to listen and draw from the unique perspective their wives have. This is God's design and will bring a couple's life together to a higher level.

The biggest hindrance to a man drawing out his wife's wisdom is pride. There is a powerful illustration of this in 1 Samuel 25. Abigail was a beautiful and sensitive woman married to a man named Nabal. Although Nabal was very wealthy, the Bible tells us he was crude and mean. In fact, his name means "dolt," or a stupid man.

David, who was to be Israel's next king, had voluntarily protected Nabal's men while they were shearing sheep. So David sent greetings to Nabal and asked if he would share his provisions with David and his men since they watched over Nabal's men when they were celebrating.

Nabal's answer reflected his character: "Who is David?" he said. "Should I take my provisions and share them with a bunch of outlaws? The answer is no, David. Leave me alone." (See 1 Samuel 25:10–11.) Everyone knew David since he was such a mighty warrior, so Nabal's response reflected his name.

When Nabal's reply got back to David, it made him so mad he gathered four hundred of his men and said, "This dude is about to die." His pride rose up because he had been so utterly disrespected, and he was going to do something about it.

But Abigail was a wise woman, even though she was married to a jerk. When she heard of what her husband had done she loaded donkeys with provisions to meet David as he came.

Abigail knew that when men get angry and ready to fight, they don't always think straight. When she met David, she bowed down and approached him with great respect. (This is important for women to understand. If you want your husband to listen you need to be respectful when speaking to him.) Abigail then began to reason with him, saying, "My husband is wicked and ill-tempered. I am married to a stupid man. Please don't do this. I know your destiny is to become the king, and this will be a blot on your record that you don't need." (See 1 Samuel 25:23–31.)

Her demeanor calmed David, and her wisdom changed his mind. He laid down his pride and received the wisdom this woman brought him. The Bible says David replied to Abigail, "Praise the LORD, the God of Israel, who has sent you to meet me today!" (1 Sam. 25:32, NLT). "And blessed be thy advice, and blessed be thou, which hast kept me this day from coming to shed blood, and from avenging myself with mine own hand" (1 Sam. 25:33, KJV).

Notice that David blessed her because she came to *meet* him. She came to oppose him, or to respectfully give him another perspective. She came with an opposite opinion. David was wise enough to listen to her, and blessed her for her wise advice.

David took that advice and left Nabal alone. That night Nabal partied and got drunk. When he was hung over the next morning, Abigail told him about what David had planned to do to him and all his men. He had a massive stroke and ten days later died.

When David heard of this he sent a messenger to ask if Abigail would be his bride. Abigail's wisdom changed her life; she went from a miserable marriage to the wife of the man anointed king.

Here is the point. Women can frustrate men with the way they think and communicate so differently, but *different is good*! God gave us these wonderful wives to bring a perspective and a wisdom that we men need and could never find on our own. Women's often opposing viewpoints were designed to bring better perspective and help their husbands clarify situations.

You may not always agree with your wife's perspective, but recognize that God has given you an important ally in your wife. Lay down your pride and really listen to her. Most people listen for only fifteen seconds or so before interrupting the other person. Show your wife that you cherish the gift you've been given by allowing her to say her peace without interrupting her or zoning out.

We have established that women notice the details. This is how the female brain is constructed. Men need to understand these inner workings if they are going to have effective communication. But what about women? They need to understand some things about the male mind too if they are going to communicate effectively.

Men are headliners. Men like you to get to the point. For the most part, they don't need as many details as the woman. When discussing something with your husband, try to cut through the clutter. Get to the point of what you want to discuss and don't expect your husband to communicate like a woman.

Men are fixers. When a woman talks, it de-stresses her. That's why a woman will talk about things that are bothering her. Men aren't like that. When a man hears a problem from his wife, it has the opposite effect. He gets stirred up and goes into "fixer mode." He wants to do something to solve the problem. And if his wife starts to cry, which may make her feel better, he really gets worked up. He'll want to do *anything* to make it stop. This is because he cares about his wife and doesn't want her to hurt.

So here is a little tip, ladies. If you just need to talk to your husband and you are not looking for him to fix the problem, just tell him up front: "I need to talk to you about something, but I don't want you to fix anything. I just need you to listen." This will help keep him from getting stressed when you just need to talk.

One other critical aspect of good communication is listening well. I know this can be tricky, especially for men, so here are a few tips for becoming a better listener.

1. You can't listen and do something else at the same time. Shut out all distractions (TV, computer, phone) and concentrate on your spouse and what that person is saying.

2. Make eye contact. The eyes are the window to the soul. Looking into your spouse's eyes will connect you on a deeper level.

3. Listen to how your spouse feels. For the most part when men and women communicate, women will often say, "This is how I *feel* about what you are saying" while men will say, "This is what I *think* about what you are saying." Women, don't dismiss what your husband says because he doesn't seem to be sharing his feelings. And husbands, don't overlook your wife's emotions to focus on solving the problem. Each of you, in your own way, must try to hear your spouse's heart.

FIGHT FAIR

No matter how well you master these communication skills the truth is, there will still be conflict from time to time. Men and women each have their own unique way of thinking. Remember, as we discussed in chapter 1, that after Eve came on the scene the words for man and woman came from Hebrew letters that create the word picture "fire."[10] Without God in the center of a marriage, this fire can be destructive. But fire that is harnessed is a source of power and blessing.

In too many Christian marriages the fire God gave us is burning down our homes because we don't know how to handle disagreements. So I want to close this chapter with some practical tips on how to deal with conflict when it arises so your passion doesn't burn your house down.

1. Realize that conflict is not bad.

Getting things out in the open will bring clarity and understanding to your relationship. We knew a couple who had been married for over forty years. At one point they went to visit their adult daughter, and she noticed her mom couldn't say a civil word to her dad. Her mom was constantly critical about everything he did. After a few hours of this, she asked her mom, "Mom, what's wrong? Why are you being so critical of Dad?"

Her mom opened up and told her that she always felt like her husband put his mother before her. His mother had lived with them when they were first married, and it had caused some conflict but she never told her husband about it. Her mother-in-law had been dead for years, but her buried frustration had made her bitter and for some reason that bitterness was now coming to the surface.

The daughter asked her, "Have you ever told Dad about this?" She said, "No, he wouldn't care." The daughter said, "Mom, you owe it to Dad to tell him how you feel and give him a chance to fix it."

That night the daughter brought her parents together and led her mother in sharing how she felt. As the mother explained to her husband that she felt he had put his mother before her, he began to cry like a baby. He said, "I never knew you felt that way. I am so sorry. Please forgive me. I will spend the rest of my life making this up to you."

They dealt with that issue, and they said the next two decades of their marriage were the best of their lives. But they didn't have to wait so long. They wasted years of happiness by not dealing with a problem in their relationship.

Don't allow bitterness in your marriage. Don't allow things to fester and time to pass without communicating about the issues that hurt you. Days can become weeks, and weeks become months and then years. Hurt turns into bitterness that has the power to destroy your life. Ephesians 4:27 says, "Neither give place to the devil." We give the devil a place in our lives when we don't deal with things and instead let them fester and produce death. Even if it's uncomfortable, deal with conflicts when they arise. Keep open lines of communication.

2. Don't attack the person, attack the issue.

The goal when you disagree is not to determine who is right or wrong. The goal is to resolve the issue. The devil wants to get in the middle of your disagreement and paint your spouse as your enemy. Remember, your spouse is your ally. Deal with the issue you are disagreeing about without turning against your spouse.

3. Discipline the way you disagree.

Don't belittle your mate, or use cutting remarks, negative body language (rolling eyes), emotional threats, or obscenities. People get into bad habits and lose all control when a disagreement comes up. You are a Christian. The Holy Spirit is there to help you argue without being ugly toward each other. You can stop ugly behavior by the power of the Holy Spirit.

4. Stick to the subject.

Keep the past in the past. Avoid phrases like "you always do this." Don't be a history buff. Remember Philippians 3:13, "But I focus on this one thing: forgetting the past and looking forward to what lies ahead" (NLT).

5. When you can't come to a place of resolution, take a time-out.

It may take thirty minutes or it may take a few hours, but it can be good to get alone and process. Let God speak to you about the situation. He may cause you to see the situation differently, or He may help you better understand your spouse's point of view. Even if you need some alone time, always come back together. Don't let walls build that separate you.

I have a pastor friend who says it this way: "My wife and I live by the cheek to cheek rule. When we go to bed at night we are either touching cheeks face to face or touching cheeks back to back." What he's saying is that even if you need to take a time-out, don't withdraw from your spouse. Don't refuse to touch and be touched by your spouse, even if you're working through a disagreement. God has designed human touch as an important part of your marriage. Touch is a way we stay connected to each other. Sexual touch is a part of that, but holding hands and cuddling are important too. Don't give the devil room to get in by refusing to touch.

Even when you've done everything you know to do to argue constructively, some disagreements will leave you feeling hurt and angry. In those times you must choose to forgive. Unforgiveness can be costly. I'll illustrate with this story.

Years ago Trudi had a disagreement with a close acquaintance. She admits to holding some resentment. One day at church the pastor preached on unforgiveness and the effects holding on to grudges and bitterness can have on you. That day Trudi made a conscious decision to forgive and let the offense go.

A few days later she was at home with the kids one morning after I had gone to work. Our children were small at that time. Brooke was four and Joshua was less than a year old and had just begun crawling well.

Trudi was cleaning up in the kitchen when she looked around to check on Josh. He was not in the kitchen, and she suddenly thought about the fact that Brooke had been taking a bath. She ran down the hall to the bathroom and there was Joshua. He had pulled himself up and managed to fall into the bathtub. It was still full of soapy water, and Josh was just sitting there with bubbles all over his little head, just looking around.

Trudi grabbed him up and held him, even though his pajamas were soaking wet. She began to cry, realizing that her baby was fine and had not drowned.

As she held him she heard Brooke say, "Mommy, it looked like somebody sat him up." He had fallen headfirst into the tub but was sitting up. Trudi knew that an angel had saved our son's life. Then she heard the Holy Spirit say, "Because you forgave it released you to be sensitive today. It caused you to check on your baby in time. It caused My power to be able to work for you."

What if Trudi had been so preoccupied by negative thoughts that it kept her from thinking to check on him? Unforgiveness will cost you. People will do you wrong in life. This is the nature of human beings. In marriage, in our family, with people in the church and the world we must forgive. Jesus forgave us when we didn't deserve it. As Christians, we must do the same. We have to be willing to let things go. Give your hurts to Jesus and don't allow bitterness and unforgiveness to poison you. It is just too great a price to pay. In the next two chapters we will continue to dig into how we can communicate more effectively by exploring the different needs we have as men and women. Not understanding our differences is probably the core reason the enemy is able to get in our house. So let's look at the top three needs of men and women so we can close the door on the enemy and devil-proof our house.

Chapter 4

UNDERSTANDING HIS NEEDS

ONE OF THE chief ways Satan gets in and attacks our marriages is when couples aren't meeting each other's needs. Understanding the top needs of men and women and how to respond to these needs in a biblical way can help keep the enemy from creating a wedge between you and your spouse. Let's begin by taking a look at the top three needs of men.

Need #1: respect

When men meet each other for the first time, usually early on in the conversation one of them will ask the other, "What do you do?" Women are different. They connect on a more relational level. They tell each other, "That blouse is adorable," or, "I love your hair." I have never had a man tell me he loved my hair, and I am fine with that.

Men ask each other what they do because they often find their identity in their work. God gave men a deep need to accomplish something in life. In order for a man to be happy he needs to feel productive by putting his hand to something and being successful at it.

Of course, we are more than what we do. Too many men (and women) fall into the trap of performance-based living. No one is more loved by God because of what he does or how well off he is. God loves everybody, often despite our performance. True success does not come because a person is rich or famous and has accomplished a lot in the eyes of man. True success is found in our faithfulness to obey God and do what He has called us to do. We were put on the earth to fulfill God's plan, and when we do so, true respect will follow.

But no matter how much attention a man puts into his work, the person he needs respect from the most is his wife. This lines up with what the Apostle Paul wrote:

> Wives, be submissive to your own husbands as unto the Lord. For the husband is the head of the wife, just as Christ is the head and Savior of the church, which is His body. But as the church submits to Christ, so also let the wives be to their own husbands in everything.
>
> —EPHESIANS 5:22–24, MEV

When a wife submits to her husband it meets his great need to be respected. But that brings up another question. What is this submission the Bible talks about?

Through the years I have heard submission taught in error. I once heard a man teach that submission meant a woman was to do whatever her husband wanted. He said even if the husband was verbally or even physically abusive, the wife was supposed to bear up under it and submit to him because this was what God wanted and He would somehow bless the situation.

That's baloney. God would never ask a woman to allow a man to whip up on her for some supposed higher purpose. In fact, if a man is abusing a woman physically that is against the law and that man should be put in jail! If you are in a marriage and you are being physically or emotionally abused, you need to get away from that person.

Submission doesn't mean wives allow themselves to be abused. So what does submission mean? Let's break the word down. The first part is the prefix "sub." Sub means to be under. A submarine goes under the water. Subterranean means to be under the surface of the earth. So we could say that submission means a woman is called to be under a mission.

But think about the word *mission*. A mission refers to an important goal or a defined purpose. In marriage this means the wife is to be under the mission God has called her and her husband to. She is to work in partnership with and under her husband's leadership. Together they pursue the family's purposes and goals together.

Every marriage is called by God to fulfill a higher purpose in the world. That's why you're here. You are a team.

The husband is the leader. It is his job to define to his wife what the goals of their marriage are and how they are to achieve them. That doesn't mean the man is a dictator and whatever he says is law. The husband needs his wife's opinion and input; he needs to listen to her. Couples won't always see eye to eye, but they must work together as a team.

The real key to biblical submission is that the husband is to lead his wife like Jesus leads His church. Notice Ephesians 5:22 says the wife is to submit to her husband "as to the Lord." This puts the heat on the man. Submission works best when the husband is reflecting the leadership of Jesus Christ. Think about how Jesus leads His church. Does Jesus ever abuse the church? Would Jesus talk down and belittle the church? You know the answer.

"But Brother Ken," you may be thinking, "I'm not Jesus. I'm not a perfect leader like Him." That's very true. But He lives in you. As you walk with Him, His power will transform you to become more and more like Him. That's what the following verse is talking about.

> And all of us, as with unveiled face, [because we] continued to behold [in the Word of God] as in a mirror the glory of the Lord, are constantly being transfigured

> into His very own image in ever increasing splendor and from one degree of glory to another; [for this comes] from the Lord [Who is] the Spirit.
>
> —2 CORINTHIANS 3:18, AMP

When husbands submit to Jesus, the Holy Spirit makes them more like Christ, and that is what causes them to grow to be good family leaders. We are all in a place of growth.

You will mess up at times. We all do. We're human. When you make a mistake, tell Jesus and your wife you are sorry. Thank God for forgiveness and the ability to start over. This is the way a true husband and leader is supposed to live.

I believe many women want to submit to their husbands, but they are frustrated because he is not clearly communicating a vision for their family. When a husband is not leading, it makes it hard for the wife to submit. On the other hand, women need to understand no man is perfect.

Even if your husband isn't living up to the standard set in Scripture, wives can still show their respect for their husbands by not criticizing him and constantly bringing up the past, not gossiping about him to others or belittling or making fun of him (especially in front of your children), and by letting him know how much you value him and what he does for your family.

When a man knows his wife respects him even when he misses it, it will give him a strength to get up and try again that nobody but his wife could supply. So let's say it this way: Man's greatest need is for his wife to respect him. But if a man is going to receive respect and submission from his wife, he has to put his big boy pants on and become the leader he's supposed to be.

If a man will properly lead his wife, most of the time the wife will follow her husband. I say most of the time because women, just like men, have the ability to make their own decisions. In observing marriages through the years, I have seen some wives refuse to follow and submit to good Christian men, even though they did their best to serve Christ and be leaders in their homes. Though the husband did all he could do, the marriage ended in divorce. No one can control another person's will. But for the most part when a man will step up and lead his marriage for Christ, his wife will follow and respect Him.

Need #2: companionship

A man's second greatest need is companionship. Men marry because they want someone to do life with. Men have a great need to connect. They want someone to support them. Men need a best friend.

One of the big reasons I was attracted to Trudi was the fun we had. In high school I was voted most friendly. I liked to make people laugh, and I loved to have a good time. I loved that Trudi laughed at my corny jokes. We began our relationship as friends who had fun together, and it escalated to romance.

It is very important to your marriage that you and your spouse are best friends. Often men fall into affairs because they're seeking companionship. Men need someone to talk to who shows them respect and believes in them. I can attest to the fact that Trudi's belief in me during the tough times of life—the times I've failed and felt so bad about myself—has been the juice that caused me to keep getting up to try again.

You don't need a soul mate outside your marriage. You need to continually work on making your spouse your best friend.

It is important that you find things you enjoy doing with your spouse. For instance, Trudi and I both love good coffee. Our house has a wet bar that we converted into an espresso bar. I bought an expensive espresso maker, and every morning we're home we start our day with some of the best lattes you've ever had. It's something we enjoy doing together.

I also have a 1987 Ford F-150 pickup truck that was my dad's before he passed away. I keep it in really good condition. It is my runaround vehicle and brings back memories. Every time I get in it, I'm reminded of my dad. It has that big 1980s seat and is actually very comfortable. I installed a new sound system and we use its Bluetooth technology to listen to music through my phone. Trudi and I have dates in the truck. We'll put on some sixties music, get a cup of coffee, and just drive around and enjoy each other's company. It's something we both enjoy and that we can do together.

We also need to study our spouse and be willing to do the things the other person likes even if it's not our favorite activity. Trudi loves to go the mall and spend hours doing what she calls shopping. She can go to the mall and look around for hours without buying anything. When I shop I pretty much know what I want when I leave the house. I go straight to the store that carries the item, and I buy it if I think the price is right. But I still go "shopping" with Trudi because I love her and want to be involved in the things she loves. She, in turn, goes to movies I want to see and restaurants she knows I prefer, because it's important to us to spend time together and share our likes with each other.

Of course it is good for couples to have friends other than their spouse. But it is not a good idea for friends to do a better job of meeting your spouse's need for companionship than you do.

It is critical to your marriage that you and your spouse get away from the pressures of life and enjoy each other. You need to laugh and make sure you are having fun together. The joy of the Lord produces new strength for the journey.

The Jewish people were mandated by God to keep the Sabbath (Exod. 20:8). The Sabbath represented one day every week when they were to do no work. It was a day for them to be thoughtful and thankful for God and His blessing in their lives. It was also a day to physically rest, pull back from the pressures of life, and have fun with their families.

When Trudi and I visited Israel, we observed the Sabbath. Not all Jewish people observe the Sabbath today, but many still do. It begins on Friday when the sun goes down and lasts until nightfall the next day. Whether families stay at home or go away to a hotel, they spend the Sabbath fellowshipping, studying the Torah, and resting.

God instituted the Sabbath in the beginning when He rested on the seventh day after He created the earth in six days. This was also the fourth commandment given to Moses. As Christians we are not under the law to keep the Sabbath, but the principle of the Sabbath still holds true today. God instituted the weekly Sabbath so that every week people would rest and remember that life was about more than living by human effort. God wanted us to be reminded that we need to put our trust in Him and not ourselves.

Jesus came to be our Sabbath. He came to be our rest. God doesn't want us to be workaholics and kill ourselves scratching out a living. Yes, we are to work, but we also are supposed to trust in the grace and blessing of God. We need to learn to rest in His promise and be sure we are enjoying life together in our marriage and with our children. Make a commitment to never stop having fun in your family, even during the difficult times.

Need #3: sex

The third greatest need in a man's life is sex. This is probably no surprise. Sex holds a very high and unique place in men's lives. I read about a recent survey that discovered the days men most like to make love. It was interesting that the preferred days all began with a T: Tuesday, Thursday, today, tomorrow, Taturday, and Tunday.

You get the point. Sex is a big deal to men. It's a driving force for men that has physiological roots. I believe the desire for sex speaks to a man's need to reproduce himself and achieve goals in life. I am not saying that women don't enjoy sex, but women view sex differently. Women have physical needs too, but they crave attention and affection as much as a man craves sex. They want to be touched, but not just sexually. When a man will take the time and care to be tender and loving toward his wife with nonsexual touch, it makes his wife more open to physical intimacy.

The act of sex also has very different effects on men and women. When a woman experiences intimate touch or sexual intimacy with a man, a chemical called oxytocin is released in her bloodstream and bathes her brain. This is a bonding hormone. It is the same hormone that is released in her body when she has a baby. Oxytocin causes her to bond and connect to her baby at birth and is reenergized during the process of breast feeding.[1]

This hormone acts as an agent to mentally connect the woman to the man and cause her to bond with him. The male is a little bit different. When a man engages in sex, vasopressin is released. This chemical acts as a bonding agent too, but the bonding process is different in a male. This chemical creates a desire in the male to repeat the sexual activity. This is the reason men can have sexual relations with a woman and just walk away while women have a stronger emotional tie to one man. This is also the reason a woman will stay with a man even if he is hateful and abusive.[2]

Sex is an important part of being joined together in marriage and must be honored. The Bible tells us we are made of three parts: spirit, soul, and body (1 Thess. 5:23). Marriage is the only relationship ordained by God to unite people on all three levels.

You are united spiritually when you enter into the marriage covenant before God.

You are united mentally when you learn the differences in the ways men and women think, and commit to listen to each other and draw from your unique perspectives. This is a lifelong learning process.

You are united physically when you have sexual relations. The two become one.

You could also say it this way: There is a mental part of your marriage, a physical part, and a spiritual part. If you are going to have a complete and mature marriage relationship, you must honor and develop all three areas.

Sex is designed to be the physical act that unites a man and woman in this holy thing called marriage. Sex outside of marriage, in any form, is sin. The Book of Proverbs warns again and again for men to keep themselves from the immoral woman. This is a metaphor for the many ways sin tempts us. But a big part of the deception Satan uses, particularly for men, is sexual temptation.

When it comes to being tempted sexually, men and women, for the most part, are aroused very differently. I say for the most part because this is not always true, but generally speaking, men are primarily stimulated visually. The image of the female body has an immediate effect on a man. It's not that the male image doesn't move a woman, but it is not quite the same.

You could say it this way: men are like microwave ovens. They heat up and are running the second the button is pushed. Women are more like crock pots. It takes some time and simmering for things to develop.

Because seeing the female body has such an instant effect on men, Satan sees to it that it is flaunted in our society constantly. Sex sells. That's why so many television commercials, from razor blades to pickup trucks, use scantily clad women to target the male audience. Those images instantly get a man's attention because of the way he is wired. Ads targeting women don't use scantily clad men in the same way ads targeting men do.

Typically, women respond to the hero image. That's why macho images like Mr. Clean are used to sell household cleaner.

One of the primary weapons Satan is using to slowly and deliberately destroy men's lives is sexual sin. It is epidemic in our time. Adultery and pornography, whether soft or hard, are ravaging single and married men, young and old, and unfortunately Christians are no exception.

Unbridled lust in any form is very destructive. Look at what the Scripture declares:

> For their command is a lamp and their instruction a light [this speaking about God's Word]; their corrective discipline is the way to life. It will keep you from the immoral woman, from the smooth tongue of a promiscuous woman. Don't lust for her beauty. Don't let her coy glances seduce you... Can a man scoop a flame into his lap and not have his clothes catch on fire? Can he walk on hot coals and not blister his feet?
>
> —PROVERBS 6:23–25, 27–28, NLT

You may be thinking, "This is talking about someone who is involved in prostitution. I would never go to a prostitute. I just look at a little pornography from time to time." The effects are the same! Sexual perversion in any form is designed to get its tentacles in you. It is addictive and overpowering. It wants to take you down a slow path that will destroy your marriage, your family, and eventually your life. The last verses use the illustration of fire and hot coals.

What if someone tied you up and put flaming hot charcoal on your chest? Could you survive that? If the coals were removed fast enough, you probably could. But the longer they lay on your chest, the deeper and uglier the scars would be. And if left long enough they would eventually kill you in the most painful death you could imagine.

The Word of God lets us know that unbridled lust and sexual sin temptations aren't freeing; they're a hellish prison you enter that eventually kills you and can even take you to hell! Dealing with lust is essential. The longer you wait the more damage is inflicted. Look at what the Scriptures say:

> Her feet [the immoral woman, unbridled lust] go down to death; her steps take hold on hell.
>
> —Proverbs 5:5, kjv

> Her house [the immoral or strange woman, unbridled lust] is the way to hell, going down to the chambers of death.
>
> —Proverbs 7:27, kjv

Porn is serious business. It is insidious and addictive. The big problem, though, is that you can't just get rid of your God-given drive for sex. It's not like the alcohol addiction I once struggled with. You've already read that before I was twenty years old, I was drinking on a daily basis. I've heard stories about people who have been instantly delivered from alcohol addiction and never struggled with it after they met Christ. It didn't work that way for me. I had a life-changing encounter with Jesus, but I continued to struggle with drinking. I knew God wanted me to quit drinking alcohol, and I felt guilty every time I would drink again, but I couldn't seem to stop. I didn't drink quite as much, but I continued to fall to the temptation. This went on for about a year.

One day Trudi went to the doctor to get a routine physical. During the mammogram they found a spot that they were concerned about. They called her and set an appointment to do a second examination. I was very concerned and felt a deep conviction about my inability to get the victory over my drinking issues. I went to the Lord and told Him, "Lord, I've failed many times. But I'm telling You today, if You will take care of Trudi, my drinking days are over. By Your grace, I walk away from drinking the rest of my life right now."

I gathered up all the beer and liquor I had in the house (the fact that I kept it around tells you I wasn't really serious about not drinking), poured it out, and threw the bottles and cans away. I meant business. I've heard people say you can't make deals with God. All I know is that when I made that vow that day, I sensed that something changed.

Trudi came home from the examination with a clean report. Nothing was there. After that, temptation would still try to come. I remember going to convenience stores and walking by the cold cases full of beer. I would look at the beer and nearly break out in a cold sweat. It was pulling me, but I kept right on walking. As time passed, the images bothered me less. It took some time but things changed. I have been free from alcohol now for forty-three years. I can look at beer at a convenience store now and it doesn't affect me at all. The temptation is gone.

But sex is not that way. You don't want to be totally delivered from sexual desire. God designed it to be a big part of your married life. So you have to learn to deal with it in the proper way, which means you are going to have to learn to manage sexual temptation when it comes. Doing so is serious business.

Maybe you are reading this and you are dealing with lust or even sexual addiction. Let me give you some practical steps to get free.

Go to God.

Pray. Confess your sin to the Lord. God is merciful and compassionate. Jesus didn't come to condemn, He came to set the captives free. Thank God for the cleansing blood of Jesus. God does and will forgive you (1 John 1:9), even if you fail and fall many times. His mercies are new every morning (Lam. 3:22–23).

Get in His Word and go to a church that believes in the power of Jesus Christ to heal and transform. It is the Word of God that will empower you to overcome.

Become accountable to another person.

Tell somebody. Sometimes it is not enough to just confess to God. You may need outside help. You may be ashamed and embarrassed to ask for help, but if you are continually going to God and repenting only to fall again and again, you need someone to stand with you. Choose someone you trust who is spiritually mature—your pastor, your spiritual mentor, or maybe your father or a good Christian friend. James 5:16 tells us, "Confess your sins to each other and pray for each other so that you may be healed" (NLT).

Tell your spouse.

I know this is a tough one. Your spouse is probably the one person you *don't* want to find out about your secret. I can't promise you that your spouse won't get angry with you or even leave, but hear me out.

I counseled a young man who had a strong addiction to pornography. He was a youth pastor in a church, and when it was discovered he was using porn he was fired from his job. Of course, his wife also found out and was devastated. Women take their husbands looking at pornography as a personal rejection. They often think, "He is doing this because I am not pretty enough." But the issue is not the wife's beauty. It is not about the wife at all. This young man's wife was beautiful. Pornography is designed by the devil to take men into a fantasy world that doesn't really exist. No real person could ever measure up to the fantasy created by pornography.

This young man really wanted to be free. That's the key. You have to want it. He began a process of obtaining freedom. And when his wife saw his heart to genuinely change, she returned home to give him another chance.

But freedom is not just a one-time prayer. True freedom takes time and commitment. This young man wanted to be held accountable. Sometimes the temptation to view porn was so strong he would have anxiety attacks. When that would happen he would call me and I would talk him down and pray with him. As he prayed, the anxiety would slowly leave.

His wife, who was so hurt and rejected in the beginning, began to help him too. When the attacks would come he would tell her about them, and instead of feeling offended by his desire to view porn, she would pray for him. It took some time, but after a few months he began to gain some traction. It wasn't perfect, but he put the checks and balances in place that brought victory. Now he's free of that addiction, and he says the key to his win was the support of his wife.

When she would pray for him during those times of desperate temptation, it comforted him and gave him a strength to overcome unlike anything or anyone else. She made a tough choice. Instead of feeling resentment and anger, she laid her feelings and insecurities aside to help her husband in his great temptation. But she was able to do this because she saw that her husband really wanted freedom. They both walked it out. Today they have a great marriage, three beautiful children, and they pastor a growing church. Because they chose to overcome together, they have an even stronger marriage, and they have been able to help many couples who face the same challenge they did. In fact, his wife is a budding writer and has in her heart to write a book for the wives of men who are facing this issue.

What the devil meant for destruction was turned into blessing because they chose to overcome together. Because of the effects of pornography in our society, there are many excellent Christian resources that can help you in your pursuit of freedom.[3] If you find yourself in the throes of porn addition, total deliverance is available to you.

God designed sex. It is a very good thing. It's not bad, but it is a fire that must be contained. That is why sex is blessed *only* within the bounds of marriage. Living together is not sanctioned in the Bible and will produce judgment. Hebrews 13:4 says, "Marriage is honourable in all, and the bed undefiled: but whoremongers and adulterers God will judge" (KJV).

Sex inside of marriage is like a fire in a fireplace. But when that fire goes outside the confines of the fireplace, it can totally burn your house down. Proverbs 6:27 tells us, "Can a man scoop a flame into his lap and not have his clothes catch on fire?" (NLT).

God created us to enjoy a fulfilling sexual life in our marriage. The Bible tells us that Adam and Eve "were both naked and were not embarrassed or ashamed in each other's presence" (Gen. 2:25, AMP). Couples need to be open with each other and discover what does and doesn't work in their intimacy.

The devil will use our God-given desire for sex to separate us from our spouse. That's why I encourage couples not to deprive each other sexually. When two people marry, they are making a covenant to share *everything,* including their bodies. The Apostle Paul wrote:

> But because there is so much sexual immorality, each man should have his own wife, and each woman should have her own husband. The husband should fulfill his wife's sexual needs, and the wife should fulfill her husband's needs. The wife gives authority over her body to her husband, and the husband gives authority over his body to his wife.
>
> —1 Corinthians 7:2–4, NLT

So one key in devil-proofing your marriage is understanding a husband's needs. Husbands, guard yourself in these areas. And wives, make it a priority to respect your husband, find ways to enjoy time with him, and be physically intimate with him. When you do, you will build a safeguard around your relationship that the enemy won't be able to easily penetrate.

Chapter 5

UNDERSTANDING HER NEEDS

Now that we've looked at men's needs, let's take a look at the top three needs of women. There is some overlap, but for the most part, you'll see that women's needs are quite different.

Need #1: security

The number one need of a wife could be expressed in the word security. A woman wants to know that a man is going to love and accept her, watch over her, care for her, support her, and provide for her and the children they have. The kind of security women seek is not only material. It involves spiritual leadership, emotional support, and physical protection along with financial provision.

Many women are working and some are earning more than their husbands. In fact, according to the Pew Research Center, four in ten American households with children under the age of eighteen now include a mother who is either the sole or primary wage earner of the family. This number has quadrupled since 1960.[1]

But even in this post-feminist era, many women still long to be doted on, watched over, and yes, provided for by a hero husband.[2] Women have a deep desire to be cherished, which is why God told husbands, "Love your wives, just as Christ also loved the church and gave Himself for her, that He might sanctify and cleanse her with the washing of water by the word" (Eph. 5:25–26, NKJV).

What women are looking for in their husbands is true love, and that is defined by sacrifice. In the New Testament, there are four different Greek words translated "love." Each describes a different aspect of love and how it works in relationships.

Phileo is the Greek word for friendship. It describes two people who are comrades or buddies with each other.

Storge describes the love a parent would have for his child. It points to a deeper relationship than *phileo*.

Eros is the word for erotic love. It could describe the sexual relationship God has ordained for marriage.

Agape is the deepest kind of love. It is not based on feelings or physical attraction, despite what Hollywood tells us. The best word to describe *agape* is sacrifice and is best described in John 3:16: "For God so loved the world that He *gave*." God's *agape* love is not based on our performance, because we cannot deserve it. This kind of love is a gift. It is the best word to describe who God is and how He loves us (1 John 4:8).

Agape love is the kind of love wives are longing for. Yes, it is a tall order for husbands to live up to, but it is the kind of love Jesus modeled toward the church. The husband and father is supposed to lay down his life for his family.

Here's another Hebrew secret. The Hebrew word for father consists of two letters. It is interesting that these are the first two letters of the Hebrew alphabet, *alef* and *bet*.

Remember that the Hebrew language is expressive and contains word pictures. The word picture for *alef* is the ox. An ox is an animal of strength.[3] In ancient times, an ox was a burden bearer and was used for hard labor. But though oxen are hardworking, they are also very submissive, patient, and easy to lead.

The second letter in the Hebrew word for father is *bet*. You may remember that the entire Bible begins with the letter *bet*. This letter is represented by a house, which can also mean family. So when you put them together the word father means "the first strong leader of the house."[4]

This is, first of all, a picture of our God. He is more than "the big guy in the sky," or the great CEO of heaven. He is a father who wanted a family and children. That is why we exist.

"The first strong leader of the house" is also what a true husband and father is supposed to be. Just like the ox, the man is to live a life of sacrificing for the good of his family. But remember, the ox is submissive and easily led. This illustrates that a husband doesn't lead in his own strength; he follows God and is easily led by the Holy Spirit. When a man will sacrifice his life to follow Jesus first, it empowers him to properly lead his family.

Having said that, at the end of the day, a wife's security is not in her husband. We all must look to Jesus for our security. Marriage at its best is not a union of two people; it is a covenant between a husband, wife, and the Holy Spirit. The Bible says, "A person standing alone can be attacked and defeated, but two can stand back-to-back and conquer. Three are even better, for a triple-braided cord is not easily broken" (Eccles. 4:12, NLT).

Need #2: communication

The second greatest need a woman has is for communication. Women don't just need their husbands to talk to them, though that is an important first step; they need specific details. They want the finer points. I'm talking minutiae, technicalities, particulars. Men are headliners while women want to read every line and break it all down.

We've already established that clear communication is *the* key for a healthy marriage. What makes this challenging is the tremendous differences between men and women. Because of these differences, communication is something couples must work at *every day*. It doesn't just happen.

It's not like that before you get married and are still getting to know each other. I remember when Trudi was my girlfriend in high school. We used to talk on the phone a lot, but phone conversations were totally different back then.

We grew up in a rural community. Of course, these were the days before cell phones. The phone lines we used were called party lines. What that meant was that people didn't have a private line. You shared a phone line with the people who lived in your area. There might be six or eight different families on one line.

If you picked up the phone and somebody was using it, you could hear their conversation. That meant you had to wait until they hung up to use the phone. I remember as a little kid trying to sneak around to listen in on people's conversations. If I picked up the phone slowly enough, it wouldn't click very loudly and no one would know I was listening. Sometimes I got caught, but often it worked.

Because of party lines, we had a three-minute limit on our phone conversations. At the end of three minutes, there was a warning beep and then a few seconds later the call was cut off. If you wanted to continue the conversation, you had to redial.

Of course, Trudi and I wanted to talk for hours just like any other teenagers. But my parents didn't want me to talk on the phone all the time, so I wasn't supposed to call Trudi back after the three-minute limit. But Trudi and I figured out a system. We learned that after we got cut off, if one of us redialed within a few seconds (we had to time it just right), the other person could pick up the phone without it ringing. I used to wait until my parents went to sleep and sneak into the kitchen (we only had one phone and it was in the kitchen) and call her. By using this system we used to talk on the phone for *hours* without our parents knowing it.

I look back now and think, "What did we talk about for all that time?" I don't remember it all, but I do remember talking about school, each other, and our hopes and dreams for the future. I remember just loving to hear her voice and feel close to her. Looking back, I realize that time was very important.

Before you marry, communication is easy. You have so much to learn about each other. Conversation comes naturally and you don't have to work at it. But after you've been married awhile, things change. You begin to take each other for granted and don't work on communicating as much anymore. This is often where people begin to think they have fallen out of love. You don't just fall out of love. You get familiar with each other and stop working on your connection.

You have to work to keep your communication lines open. Men, realize that your wife has a great need to tell you about the details of life, and if she can't talk to you she may find someone else to talk to. She wants to connect with you through words, so you'll need to take time to listen to her and to share the details of what you're doing with her. But wives, realize your husband is not wired the way you are. Don't expect him to communicate the way you do. God made you different on purpose.

Meeting this need for communication is something couples have to work on *daily*. When Trudi and I were using that party line, we had to work at it. It wasn't always convenient. The world around us is like that party line. There are many voices that try to interfere and keep us apart. You have to work at finding time to talk and listen to each other.

The words we speak to our spouse are very important, because words are powerful. The tongue is the only muscle in the body that is attached at only one end. That says two things to me:

1. The words we use are open-ended, meaning we choose what we say.
2. The words we choose connect our marriage to either life or death because Proverbs 18:21 says,

> "Death and life are in the power of the tongue, and those who love it will eat its fruit."

As a husband, I know the words I choose to speak to and over my wife have the ability to bring life or death to her. That tells me I need to listen to her heart and wash her with words that heal, build up, and clear away the lies the devil tries to tell her. As Proverbs 15:4 declares, "A wholesome tongue is a tree of life, but perverseness in it breaks the spirit."

Wives, it's important that you also speak words of blessing over your husband. Look for something to admire about him every day. Compliment him and make an effort to tell him how much you appreciate him. And both husbands and wives should pray for each other daily. No words you speak will make a bigger impact on your marriage than words of prayer. That is why we have included several prayers to pray over your family in the Appendix.

Need #3: leadership

We discussed in the last chapter that a man needs respect, especially from his wife. But respect must be earned, and it is easiest for a wife to respect her husband when she sees him leading the family. A godly husband and father doesn't lead by being a dictator; he leads by being a follower. The greatest leaders are those who make following Jesus their priority. When a wife knows her husband is a God chaser, it produces a confidence in her to submit to the mission God has given them as a couple and as a family. And it helps to make her feel secure, which is her number one need.

We shared the story of how Trudi came to Christ before me and prayed me into the kingdom. When I was first saved I had a lot to learn. My wife was very strong spiritually. In the early days, I would defer to her when it came to spiritual matters.

She knew how to pray and hear from God better than I did, so I kind of pulled back when it came to spiritual things. I respected her as the more spiritually strong one in our marriage.

In 1975 we had our first child. We weren't supposed to have children (we will share more about this in Part 3), so we were thrilled when Trudi found out she was pregnant. But six weeks before the baby was due, Trudi had to have an emergency C-section.

This was the mid-1970s so a C-section was major surgery. Our baby girl Brooke was so tiny (four pounds, two ounces) we couldn't take her home for two weeks. When we did, the doctors told us we needed to keep her isolated. Her lungs were so fragile that a common cold could be deadly, so Trudi had to stay home for weeks watching her.

During that time Trudi became very disheartened and discouraged. She had nearly died with the toxemia before the C-section, and she was still recovering from the surgery. And now she had to deal with the pressure of watching our new baby so closely all the time and had developed a severe case of postpartum depression. All of this was taking quite a toll on her. It seemed she had lost her will to go on.

This was when I began to serve God on a deeper level. One night we had a guest speaker at our church named Dick Mills. Thank God for anointed ministers. We all need the church and anointed ministry if we are going to grow spiritually. Dick Mills was a powerful preacher who moved in the prophetic. He would pray over people, and God would give him scriptures to share with them. I think he must have had the whole Bible memorized.

When he prayed over me, the verses he gave me had to do with me being called into the ministry and God using me mightily. I really heard from God that night.

When I got home after church, I told Trudi what had happened. I told her, "God has some awesome things in store for us.

I saw it tonight. We are going to do this together. I know you're discouraged and I know you've lost some heart, but we are going to go on and obey God. I'm taking you with me, even if I have to put you on my back and piggyback you all the way!"

She says when I said that to her, she seemed to gain new strength. To know that I was leading the way and that I was not willing to leave her behind helped her turn the corner to move past the discouragement the enemy was using against her. She has been right by my side all these years, through the thick and the thin.

There will be times of victory and times you will face discouragement in your marriage. When the man steps up to the plate to lead his wife by being a follower of Christ, it will fill her with the confidence she needs to fulfill her role in the marriage.

If your husband hasn't stepped up to be a spiritual leader in your home, pray for him. Never underestimate the power of prayer. Trudi's prayers brought me into the kingdom. God works powerfully through a praying spouse.

When you pray, declare God's Word over your marriage. Declare, according to Ephesians 5:21–33, that your husband leads his home as Christ leads the church, loving you as Christ loves us and giving himself for you and your family. Declare by faith that your husband will see himself as a mighty man of valor and know that the Lord is with him (Judg. 6:2). Thank the Lord that, according to Ephesians 6:4, your husband will raise your children in the nurture and admonition of the Lord. (We have included a prayer for families in the Appendix as well as blessings husbands can speak over their wives and that wives can speak over their husbands.) Speak life into your husband and into your marriage, and trust that your prayers are making a difference even if it seems nothing is changing.

Many women feel their husbands aren't taking an active leadership role in the more practical areas of life—parenting, budgeting, and decision making. If that is happening in your home, resist the temptation to berate and criticize your husband. We know that may not be easy, but complaining won't motivate your husband to change. It will just frustrate both of you. "A wise woman builds her house, while a foolish woman tears hers down by her own efforts" (Prov. 14:1, TLB). You can tear down your husband and your marriage with your words.

Husbands need their wives to believe in them, and sometimes wives are communicating the opposite when they don't show him respect or don't let him lead. If your husband has been passive at home, be intentional about getting his input on decisions. Ask him what he thinks is best, and tell him you trust his judgment (and mean it). If things don't work out, don't berate him. Start discussing alternative solutions.

If you want to motivate your husband to lead, make suggestions not demands, and use wisdom in the way you communicate your ideas and concerns to him. We're not saying you should never disagree. You are the helper who sometimes needs to oppose. But the way you voice your disagreement is key. Couples should always approach each other with respect. (We will talk more about honoring your spouse in the next chapter.)

Invite the Holy Spirit into your marriage

God designed men and women to be different. This can be frustrating, but He did this to bring greater blessing into our lives. It's like in chemistry. When two hydrogen atoms and one oxygen atom are compounded, they create a wonderful life-giving force called water. We cannot survive without water, but this substance is created only when the right amount of hydrogen bonds with the right amount of oxygen.

Salt is another example. This life-giving compound is created only when one atom of sodium bonds with one atom of chloride. You can't take a dose of chloride and a dose of sodium and expect your body to function as it should. That won't work. Sodium and chloride in their raw forms are toxic. They could kill you. In order to produce life they must bond *before* entering your body.

In order to have a life-giving relationship that impacts God's kingdom, couples must bond together through the power of the Holy Spirit. If a couple doesn't bond properly, their relationship becomes toxic. No life is produced because there is no bonding. This bonding doesn't just happen. It is a process. It must be worked out between two people over time as they apply the truth of God's Word we have discussed in their lives and their marriage. So invite the Holy Spirit to bring the life of God into your marriage. Welcome Him into your home and into your marriage. Give Him permission to shape you into the spouse He created you to be, and ask Him to show you how to love your spouse the way He loves us. If you ask Him, the Holy Spirit will trigger the spark that will help you and your spouse bond and become one.

We've looked at many truths that, when applied, can take your marriage to new and higher levels. But we have one more principle to look at. And the application of this one can be the catalyst that will change your marriage forever.

Chapter 6

THE POWER OF HONOR IN MARRIAGE

As we conclude the section on marriage, let's do some review. Marriage is the highest human relationship you can have with another person. Marriage is the first relationship established in the Bible and is the foundation for all other relationships. The devil never showed up in the Garden of Eden until Adam and Eve got married. He saw this marriage as a threat to his plan, so he attacked it. Just as man fell from grace that day in the garden, we could also say that marriage fell from grace.

This is why Jesus came. He came to give mankind back what Adam and Eve lost. He restored us back to God, but He also restored *marriage*. Now through Christ and the application of His Word, your marriage can be redeemed, healed, and restored from anything Satan has been able to do. By continuing to grow and be willing to act you can devil-proof your marriage for the future.

Up to now we have discussed many principles that can help you have a better marriage. But in this chapter we will discuss the one ingredient that will cause everything we have talked about to work. This ingredient is honor.

In order to understand the force of honor, we must first understand what honor is. The dictionary defines honor with words such as "integrity," "worth," "merit," and "rank." It defines a man of honor as one who is honest, fair, and exhibits integrity because of his *actions*. So we could say that honor is an act. It could even be called an act of service.

But that's what the dictionary has to say. Let's see what the Bible tells us about honor in marriage.

> Likewise, ye husbands, dwell with them according to knowledge, giving honour unto the wife, as unto the weaker vessel, and as being heirs together of the grace of life; that your prayers be not hindered.
>
> —1 PETER 3:7, KJV

The word "honor" in this passage comes from the Greek term *teemay*. It is defined as "a valuing by which a price is fixed."[1] So we could say that honor is an act of evaluating something and then paying the price according to its esteemed worth.

If a husband gives honor to his wife, that would mean he would discern her value and then pay the price to give her the honor she is due. He would do that because of her value to him. The same is true of wives.

The foundation of the act of honor is love, which is why Jesus's sacrifice on the cross is the highest example of honor. John 3:16 says, "For God so loved the world that He gave His only begotten Son, that whoever believes in Him should not perish but have everlasting life" (NKJV). This is the most famous scripture in the Bible, and it should be. It defines everything about God and His attitude toward mankind.

The verse doesn't just say God loved the world. If God just loved the world that would have been enough. But it says God *so* loved the world that He gave. He acted on His love toward us by sending His Son to die on the cross for our sins. Love is a verb. It is an act. And it always costs something.

The price to redeem mankind was high. It cost God the best He had, which was His one and only Son. The Father was compelled to act because of His great love for us and His desire to get His family back. He didn't send His Son to die for us because we asked Him to do it. He certainly didn't do it because we deserved it. He did it because He loved us. It was an act of honor.

Applying honor in marriage

Let's look again at 1 Peter 3:7.

> Likewise, ye husbands, dwell with them according to knowledge, giving honour unto the wife, as unto the weaker vessel, and as being heirs together of the grace of life; that your prayers be not hindered.
>
> —KJV

This verse says the wife is the weaker vessel. While it is true that men, for the most part, are physically stronger than women, this verse goes deeper than that. As author Gary Smalley notes, the term "weaker" vessel could be read as the "more sensitive" vessel.[2] God created women with a great sensitivity, and men need the sensitivity the wife brings to the marriage.

Also notice that the wife is referred to as a "vessel." A vessel holds things. You could also say a vessel carries or transports. Let's use a vase as an example. If you, as a man, buy your wife a bouquet of roses (which I highly recommend that you do; most women love flowers and it is a great way to show them honor), you don't just lay the flowers on the counter. You put them in a vase so they can be displayed and so they can be constantly watered to preserve their life.

I've discovered different vases have different prices. You can go to a store like Walmart and buy an ordinary vase for ten dollars. But you can also go to a higher end store, like a Nordstrom or Bloomingdale's, and find pricier vases. One of the most expensive department stores in the country is Neiman Marcus.

They have some ultra-extravagant items in their catalog. When I thumbed through one recently, there were vases that cost a thousand dollars. Can you imagine paying that much for a vase?

They also had vases that cost two thousand dollars, three thousand dollars, and even more. I found one vase called the Lalique Spiral Grande Vase that sold for $16,600! When you pay that much money for a vase, the name changes! It's no longer pronounced "vase" with a long "a." It changes to "vahz," and you have to say it with a refined British accent!

What is my point? If an item is more valuable, you will treat it differently. The higher something is appraised the more you honor it.

Let's say I bought a ten dollar vase from Walmart to put some roses in. If my grandchildren were playing around in my house and the vase got broken, it would be no big deal. I can replace a ten dollar vase.

But if I bought the Lalique Spiral Grande Vase for $16,600, I promise you I would treat it totally different. I would want to put it in a prominent place in the house so everyone could see it. I *would not* put it in a place where my grandchildren might knock it over and break it. We have some sturdy shelves on the wall in our house that are twelve-feet high. I would probably hire a company that was bonded to put it on the shelf, so if they broke it, their insurance would cover it.

I would have the company secure the vase on the shelf so it couldn't move after it was placed up there, then I would buy some type of insurance to cover it in case of a natural disaster or theft. When my friends came over I would proudly show it to them. I would say, "Do you see that vase up there? That is Lalique Spiral Grande Vase. That sucker cost me $16,600. That is not a vase. Repeat after me in a British accent, that is a *vahz*! Let's stand here and admire this thing for a while."

I would be proud of it, and I would treat it as something

precious because of its perceived value. Now, husbands, relate that vase to your wife. God gave you a very valuable treasure in her. There are many gifts in her, but in order for them to manifest they must be drawn out.

The husband's treatment of his wife determines if these gifts in all their richness can surface. If you don't assess your wife's worth as precious and don't draw out her inestimable value by treating her with honor, you may never uncover all the gifts and treasures God has invested in her.

If you just treat her as ordinary, that is what you will receive from her. Just ordinary. That's the way most marriages operate. Just ordinary. But you can change it if you will begin to treat her with honor. Your willingness to honor her will determine *everything* about the release of the wealth she contains. Look at what God's Word tells us about this:

> He who finds a wife finds a good thing, and obtains favor from the Lord.
>
> —Proverbs 18:22

> Houses and riches are an inheritance from fathers, but a prudent wife is from the Lord.
>
> —Proverbs 19:14

> Who can find a virtuous woman? For her worth is far above rubies.
>
> —Proverbs 31:10, MEV

Your wife is a treasure. She is more valuable than houses and riches. She is a good thing in your life! Her value is *far* above rubies. She is much more valuable than the Lalique Spiral Grande Vase. In fact, when you honor her, I believe it opens the door for you to receive all the natural benefits, things we just read about in Proverbs: good things, houses and riches, and precious rubies!

So, how can you honor your wife? Here are seven commandments:

SEVEN COMMANDMENTS FOR HONORING YOUR WIFE

1. I put no other human relationships before Trudi, including my relationship with my children.

I have other friends and mentors in life, and there are times when I need someone to talk to. But there are certain things I would never discuss with anyone but Trudi. She is my soulmate, and I constantly let her know she is number one in my life. Although I dearly love my children, my relationship with Trudi takes priority over them. If my children ever tried to sass or back talk their mother when they were growing up, I would sit them down and tell them that was a line they were never to cross. I let them know, even when they were small, that they were going to respect their mother and I would not put up with them doing otherwise. I always let them know that mama came before them. It's called being a husband and father.

2. I shall never stop dating and having fun (laughing) with my wife after we get married.

Before Trudi and I were married, we were friends. I always loved to be around her because she laughed at my corny jokes and we had a good time. Life can be hard, so never lose your sense of humor. Commit to being a joyful husband and work hard at having fun, even when your heart seems to be breaking. There is strength in joy. (See Proverbs 17:22.)

3. I shall remember anniversaries and special days so I may live long in the land the Lord has given me.

You have to work at not becoming too familiar with each other. Never stop buying gifts and surprising each other. Keep things special.

4. I shall not ride in a car, eat in a restaurant, or be alone in a room with a member of the opposite sex.

The Bible says we are to abstain from even the appearance of evil (1 Thess. 5:22). Many men have fallen into sexual sin by opening this door. Keep it closed. I would rather a woman think I am rude than for her to think I am coming on to her.

5. I shall not watch, read, or expose myself to sexually explicit shows, books, movies, etc.

Pornography is the scourge of our time, and as a man I must put some guards up. I am accountable to my wife. She has permission to monitor my computer, phone, and iPad, and to look at the history of what I have been viewing. She knows I will not be offended or say, "How dare you suspect me!" I put these lines of accountability in my life for two reasons:

My flesh is not saved, and I realize I can be tempted. I know many Christian men, even preachers, who didn't have an accountability structure in place and fell into sin.

I want my wife to feel at peace and secure knowing I am accountable to her and she doesn't have to question my actions.

6. I shall remember the implications of breaking this covenant before God.

As we have learned, marriage is a holy covenant and the second priority of a man's life. It must come before your career, your ministry, your mother, and your children. Work to improve it as if it were your greatest life's work.

7. I shall be my wife's protector.

I was working in my office one day and Trudi walked in and told me to check out a message she'd just received on Facebook. She passed me her iPad and I read it.

> Hello Dear
>
> What a nice and sparkling smile. I wouldn't trade that smile for anything. I was searching for an old friend when I stumbled on your profile. I got entangled in that wonderful smile, couldn't stop myself from saying hello.... You sparked an interest to me. Let me know if you would like to continue communicating. Do have a blissful day.
>
> Carl

This guy was boldly using Facebook to come on to my wife. I told Trudi to let me answer the guy. I got on her Facebook account and wrote:

> Hello Carl,
>
> This is Trudi's husband. She told me about you, and I just had to answer your request myself. When it comes to trading her smile, it is not your choice since it doesn't belong to you in the first place. I'm sure you checked out her profile and discovered she is married to me and we are both ministers of the gospel of Jesus Christ, which means you are way out of bounds trying to talk to my wife this way.
>
> I hope you are not a married man or claim to be a Christian yourself, because if you are, you need to repent and get right with God.
>
> Sincerely,
>
> Pastor Ken Blount

The Bible tells me I am supposed to love everybody, and I will be obedient to do so. But walking in love does not mean I will be passive in protecting my wife against predators. If someone tries to harm or abuse my wife, I am going to protect her, even if that means using force. I am committed to protecting my wife as long as I have breath in me.

Seven Commandments for Honoring Your Husband

So far, we've primarily dealt with how husbands can honor their wives, but honor is a two-way street. Now ladies, let's look at ways you can honor your husband. In this section, Trudi will share why the following practices are so important.

1. I shall communicate to my husband that I believe in him and his leadership abilities, even if he blows it.

It means everything to your husband to know that you support him, especially when things aren't going so well. In the dark times of life, make sure he knows you still believe in him when he is going through difficult seasons.

2. I shall pray for my husband and believe God is working even in the midst of his human weaknesses.

Remember our story of how I (Trudi) met Jesus before Ken did? He initially rejected Christ, and I knew that if I pushed him I would drive him away. So instead of trying to talk to him about the Lord, I talked to the Lord about him. I prayed.

As I prayed for him I began to see God's reality about him instead of the reality I was witnessing in the natural. In prayer, the Holy Spirit began showing me images of him preaching (if you could have seen him then you would know that was a miracle). The amazing thing was the more I prayed for him the bigger the crowds I saw became. In the spirit I saw him preaching to thousands of people. I have lived to see that vision come to pass.

I'm not saying that if you pray for your husband, God will make him a preacher. But praying for my husband opened the door for me to see him the way God saw him. When I saw what Jesus saw in him, it was easy for me to believe he could change.

Although Ken didn't know I was praying for him, my new-found awareness of his potential, which I saw in prayer, literally changed the atmosphere created in our home. It caused him to sense that I believed in him. When he knew that I believed in him, it softened his heart to God and helped him step up to receive Christ.

Your prayers pave the way for the Holy Spirit to deal with your husband's heart.

3. I shall not criticize my husband to others, especially my children, when I disagree with him.

Ladies, don't counsel with your children. They are not equipped to handle information about your marriage. It will create resentment from them for you and your husband.

4. I will tell my husband thank you for the things he does—providing for our family, spending time with the children, helping around the house, etc.

There is power in thanksgiving. We can become negative by concentrating on our husband's faults and not being grateful for the good things he does. But expressing our gratitude for our husbands can have the opposite effect.

Ken and I were flying to a meeting one day, and we had to sit apart on the plane. As I was sitting there on the plane, I began to think about some of the things I appreciated about him. As I thought along those lines I sensed the Holy Spirit say, "Why don't you write down twenty-five things you are thankful for and text them to him when you land?"

I began to list them:

- Thank you for being a godly man.
- Thank you for making me lattes every morning.
- Thank you for loving our children.
- Thank you for putting up with my crazy, complex personality.

I went on until I had twenty-five. When the plane landed I sent him the text and watched as he read it. He dropped his head and I could tell it touched him. It touched me more as I wrote it. Thankfulness unleashes love and healing. I challenge you to write your own list.

5. I will make him his favorite meals regularly.

I know we live in a society where both men and women work. Women these days don't necessarily do all the cooking at home. But I still believe that the way to a man's heart is through his stomach. (I know that's not in Scripture, but trust me, it's true!)

Ken loves to eat my special dishes, such as a special chocolate cake I bake. But he also enjoys certain dishes we eat at our favorite restaurants. Whatever you do, find creative ways to get him his favorite food, whether you make it or someone else does. It's one way you can make your husband feel loved and special.

6. I will be enthusiastic about our intimacy.

Women crave intimacy, but men crave sex. Remember, it came in number three on our husbands' list of needs.

The thing that makes marriage different from any other relationship you will have on the earth is the sacred act of sex. It was designed by God to keep a married couple connected. It was created to be enjoyed as the highest of covenant pleasures. Whether you experience the joys of intimacy is determined by your attitude and willingness to open up and give of yourself to your husband.

7. I will learn to communicate with him in the way he understands and not expect him to communicate the way I would.

Remember, honor is not a feeling. Honor is an act. And you may honor your spouse but not receive the same respect in return. You cannot manipulate someone into doing the right thing. But that doesn't change the fact that you must honor your spouse. Why? Because it is just right. And the honor you show will bring your spouse to a point of decision.

Remember my (Ken's) story of how Trudi's changed life opened the door for the Holy Spirit to deal with my heart when I wasn't serving Christ? After she met the Lord I never sensed any condemnation coming from her. I didn't sense that she was frustrated with me. She actually showed me more respect and honor than before she got saved. The lifestyle change she was living out before me brought me to a place of decision.

The Bible tells us this will happen:

> Likewise, ye wives, be in subjection to your own husbands; that, if any obey not the word, they also may without the word be won by the conversation of the wives.
>
> —1 PETER 3:1, KJV

The word "conversation" in this verse is not the wife's preaching. It actually refers to her behavior. It is saying a wife's Christlike behavior lived out in front of her unsaved husband will bring him to a place of conviction. God will never force anyone to receive Him, but He will work on that person's heart with the loving, convicting power of the Holy Spirit.

It is like what happened on the cross. Jesus gave His life for the sins of mankind, but He didn't make anyone accept the forgiveness He purchased. The cross is two pieces of wood joined transversely. It represents a crossroads, a place of decision. When confronted with it, people are forced to do one of two things: either accept Jesus as the way, the truth, and the life, or reject Him. The choice is always up to us.

Putting the things we have discussed into practice works the same way in your marriage. Your acting in honor will bring your spouse to a crossroads—to receive the honor shown and return that respect, or reject the biblical command to honor one's spouse. No matter what your spouse chooses, your acts of honor will force the issue.

Somebody said it this way, "It is always right to do right and always wrong to do wrong." Everything we have shared so far will do you absolutely no good whatsoever—it will profit you *nothing*—until you act. Choosing to honor your spouse and put into practice all the things you've read can change your marriage today, tomorrow, and forever.

PART III

DEVIL-PROOF YOUR CHILDREN

Chapter 7

THE DEVIL IS ALWAYS AFTER THE SEED

I HAD JUST FINISHED my sermon and handed the service back to the pastor. I had preached about what Jesus taught concerning children, which I have a strong calling to do. Before closing the service the pastor was receiving a special offering for our ministry.

"I want to encourage you to give a special gift into Brother Ken's ministry," he said. "There are many of you who have children who are away from God. We are going to pray over your gift and call this the 'children's seed.' I believe your gift today is like seed that will produce a harvest in the lives of your children. I encourage you to obey what God tells you to do financially and not hold back, because the devil is always after your seed."

His last phrase struck me that day, and I will never forget it. *The devil is always after the seed.* When you think about it, that phrase covers a lot of ground. One of the Bible's most basic and irrevocable principles for life is the principle of the seed. The Bible says, "While the earth remains, seedtime and harvest, cold and heat, winter and summer, and day and night shall not cease" (Gen. 8:22).

The principle of the seed is one of the most foundational elements to understand God's kingdom. Jesus preached about it in the parable of the sower, and after He shared the story, He asked His disciples, "Do you not understand this parable? How then will you understand all the parables?" (Mark 4:13).

Jesus was saying that if they didn't understand the principle of seedtime and harvest, they couldn't get out of first grade when it comes to comprehending His kingdom. If you are going to walk in the blessing of God on this earth you must learn that the seed you sow determines the harvest you reap.

In the church this is talked about a lot in terms of finances, like it was that day after my sermon, and this is a true financial principle. But the principle of the seed touches more than just your money. To have a good marriage you must sow seeds of love in your marriage. If you are going to have friends, you must be willing to sow seeds of friendship to others. The principle of seedtime and harvest is at work in every area of life.

But there is a seed that is more valuable and precious than the rest. Do you know what it is? Of course, we need money to live in the earth, but no matter how successful financially we might be, one day we will leave our money behind—all of it. Houses, cars, boats—no matter how shiny and pretty it is, all our "stuff" stays here on the earth at our departure. As the saying goes, "You can't take it with you."

But there is one type of seed you can take with you. That seed is our children.

Over and over the Bible likens children to seed. This began with God's covenant with Abraham.

> And I will establish my covenant between me and thee and thy seed after thee in their generations for an everlasting covenant, to be a God unto thee, and to thy seed after thee.
>
> —GENESIS 17:7, KJV

The word translated "seed" in Genesis 17:7 is used more than two hundred times in the Bible. Why is the term seed used so much? God is telling us He is multigenerational. He wants our life in Christ to not only impact us but also our children and grandchildren. We must pass it on. God told Moses:

> Perform this sign...Then they will believe that the LORD, the God of their ancestors—the God of Abraham, the God of Isaac, and the God of Jacob—really has appeared to you.
>
> —EXODUS 4:5, NLT

Jesus is called the seed of Abraham. He was able to come to the earth through succeeding generations of men who cooperated with God from generation to generation. But the devil tried to stop Jesus from the very beginning; even at His birth the devil tried to use Herod to kill Him. The devil hates God's plan. He wanted God's seed, Jesus, and he wants your kids too. The devil is always after the seed.

We must be multi-generation-minded. Because our seed, or our children, are so important, they are one of the primary targets of Satan's most strategic attacks. I was just minding my business one day when the Lord spoke a thought to me, "The devil attacks what he fears." I believe the devil's nightmare is the church waking up to see how important it is to reach the next generation for Christ.

The devil fears born-again families passing their faith down to their kids. He fears children who are trained in the Word of God growing up and living for Christ, because they will do damage to his kingdom. The devil fears you producing a legacy of faith that lives on long after you are gone. The devil hates the seed.

We mentioned that Jesus is the seed of Abraham. Why did God choose Abraham to establish His covenant? The Bible tells us:

> And the LORD said, Shall I hide from Abraham that thing which I do; seeing that Abraham shall surely become a great and mighty nation, and all the nations of the earth shall be blessed in him? For I know him, that he will command his children and his household after him, and they shall keep the way of the LORD, to do justice and judgment; that the LORD may bring upon Abraham that which he hath spoken of him.
>
> —GENESIS 18:17–19, KJV

This passage clearly tells us that God chose Abraham because he would train his children and pass the relationship God had established in him to his kids. And he did. Abraham's faith produced the nation of Israel, and it lives on today in the church of Jesus Christ! As Galatians 3:29 says, "If you are Christ's, then you are Abraham's seed, and heirs according to the promise" (MEV).

Our children are our most important legacy. We must be deliberate about training them for Christ, because the devil is certainly deliberate about attacking them.

Molech revisited

The enemy wants to keep this truth veiled, and he wants to destroy our children. The devil is always after the seed. We see this early on in God's Word. Remember the story of Joshua and the battle of Jericho? Joshua was the new leader of the nation of Israel after the death of Moses. It was his job to take the children of Israel into the Promised Land. The first battle they faced was at Jericho. The problem was that Jericho was surrounded by a wall.

This massive structure, according to archaeologists' excavations, was really a double wall. The first wall stood twelve to fifteen feet, and there was a large embankment between the first wall and the taller second wall. The entire structure appeared to be over ten stories.[1]

In the natural it was impossible to breach this wall. But God gave Joshua a plan. The Israelites marched around the walls in obedience to God's instructions, and the walls collapsed. Some theories are that a massive earthquake took place. There are even some who say the walls partially receded into the ground. Whatever happened, it was a great miracle.

But why did the walls fall in ruins? God could have just knocked a massive hole in the wall to allow the children of Israel to get in and attack. Why were the walls totally obliterated? I believe there is a reason.

The people living in Jericho were Canaanites. They worshipped an idol named Molech, the God of fire. Molech was a giant brass image with the head of a bull. In his belly was an opening where a fire burned. The way worshippers appeased this angry god was to let their children "pass through the fire" (Lev. 18:21, KJV).

This was the process. Mothers would bring their living infants before this demon God. Then at a certain point as they worshipped the idol they would roll the baby into the fire as a sacrifice! Can you imagine the screams as the babies slowly burned to death in agony? The mother was to dance and rejoice as her precious baby burned right before her eyes. If she showed any sadness or remorse her offering was not accepted.

After the babies had been burned in the fire, they would gather their ashes and put them into jars. Then they would take the jars and insert them into the walls of Jericho as a memorial to Molech. Archaeologists discovered these remains in their studies.[2] The destruction of the walls of Jericho was God's judgment against this demonic practice. It also shows us the kind of perverted madness the devil uses to destroy our children. He is serious about it.

God warned the children of Israel not to adopt the ungodly practices of the people they dispossessed when they came into the Promised Land. He specifically told them not to sacrifice their children to Molech.

> Do not permit any of your children to be offered as a sacrifice to Molech, for you must not bring shame on the name of your God. I am the LORD.
>
> —LEVITICUS 18:21, NLT

This wouldn't seem to be a difficult commandment to keep. But the Israelites later copied this practice in a valley near Jerusalem called Gehenna. How could they do this? They assimilated into the culture of the people around them. Peer pressure has always been around, and it is strong.

But that would never happen in America, right? In 1973 the Supreme Court of the United States passed legislation legalizing abortion. That was over forty years ago. Since that time, an estimated 57 million abortions have been performed in our country.[3] A number that big can kind of go over your head, so let's think about it this way. The estimated population of two of the largest states in America—California (38 million) and New York (19.7 million)—totals 57.7 million people.[4]

It's ironic that many of these aborted babies are stored in jars in abortion clinics, much like the jars in the walls of Jericho. It's Molech revisited. America is going down the same road. There is nothing new under the sun. The devil is always after the seed.

Our children are precious

Our children are precious. They are infinitely valuable, and the devil knows it. That is why every Christian needs a vision about the importance of children. I was shown this truth early in my ministry. This is how it began.

The year was 1982. It was the tail end of the time known as

the charismatic renewal and the early days of the Word-Faith movement. In April of that year, Trudi and I had moved to Tulsa. I was in the men's hairstyling business at that time, but in my heart I knew God wanted to use me in ministry.

A few months earlier I had met a man named Willie George, and we had struck up a friendship. I sensed a unique kindredness with his ministry, and he hired me to work with him. So I packed up my family and moved to Tulsa, though when I arrived it was not entirely clear what I would do. He was pastor of a church in Tulsa but also had a unique ministry designed for children. He had written a Sunday school curriculum for churches and led conferences to teach churches the importance of ministering to children.

I had been working with him just a few months when one day he called the staff (all three of us) together. He began telling us that the night before he was praying and God had clearly spoken to his heart. The Lord had instructed him to resign his position as pastor of the church and go into full-time children's ministry. The Lord told him he had to take the vision of reaching and training children to the new churches springing up all around the country and the world.

You have to understand where the church in general was at that time. In 1982, there were very few churches preaching about the power of the Holy Spirit. But there were hundreds of young pastors coming up the ranks who were planting churches all over America.

I remember sitting in that meeting thinking, "I'm glad he heard from God." Then my next thought was, "But what am I doing here, Lord? You've put doing Christian music in my heart." Before moving to Tulsa I had led worship in a church. I wanted to write songs and record music. I believed that was at the heart of my calling.

I told the Lord, "Surely You haven't called me to work with…children!"

I didn't know anything about children's ministry. Now, I didn't have anything against kids. I liked kids. I had two children I loved dearly. I used to be a kid myself. I thought kids were really cute. But ministry to children? God had called me to big-time ministry. I wanted to be respectable. God had called me to be a famous Christian music artist, not a children's minister!

In the next few months after his announcement I began traveling with Willie and assisting him. He was doing conferences in churches all over the country, teaching them how to set up and implement children's ministry in their churches and preaching to congregations about the need to reach kids with the gospel. What he shared was a revelation to the church that we must receive and embrace children's ministry if we are to fulfill our commission to preach the gospel to *all* the world. Children are a big part of the world.

In December of 1982, the same year Trudi and I moved to Tulsa, Willie and the rest of us were leading a family meeting in Houston. Part of Willie's vision was to create a television show for kids. He wanted to call it *The Gospel Bill Show*. It would be a western based in the fictional town of Dry Gulch. He would be the sheriff, Gospel Bill, and I would be his deputy-sidekick, Nicodemus. During that meeting, we used those new, developing characters in an afternoon service.

After the service we returned to the hotel. At that time, I just wasn't settled that I was in the right place, and I thought maybe I was out of the will of God for my life. I was feeling very frustrated, so I left our room and began walking around the hotel where we were staying. I was praying in the Spirit and talking to God about our situation.

I walked and prayed and prayed and walked for a little over three hours, and to be honest, I didn't feel like I had heard a thing from God. I actually felt worse and even further from God than when I started praying. Tired and frustrated, I went back up to the room and prepared to go to sleep. But when the lights went out and my head hit the pillow, I immediately sensed the presence of God come on me.

I began to weep like somebody turned on a faucet. I didn't want to disturb Willie, who I was rooming with, so I got up and went into the bathroom and closed the door.

The presence of God was so strong, I'll never forget it. As I worshipped Jesus, I saw a vision. It's the only one I've ever had all these years. I saw a giant parade. I saw ticker tape falling, bands playing, and thousands of people lining the street and hanging out the windows of huge buildings on both sides of the road. It was like film I had seen of the victory parade in New York City after World War II.

As I observed this scene I heard these words that I will never forget: "I will use you in the last days to usher in the very last praise, for the coming of the Lord is very near. You will enter into new realms of glory in these days. The key to the grand entry is the key I've given you called praise. So don't hold back but be bold, My son. There is much work left to be done. Don't let the lies of the enemy turn you aside from the vision to see."

That vision empowered me to see things in a totally different light. After that I knew I was in the right place. It was not easy (it never is when you are plowing new territory), but I traveled with Willie George to churches across the height and breadth of America in the eighties and nineties. We trained literally thousands of church workers in new full gospel churches that were being formed how to properly minister to children.

People were discovering that children's ministry is not babysitting, but when done properly children can be saved, filled with the Holy Spirit, and trained in the Word of God even though they are small. We brought a revelation about children to the body of Christ and changed the churches' concept about children. It was phenomenal. That movement still lives on in the church today. It is pretty much a given that if you are a pastor and want to draw young families, you must have a vibrant children's ministry.

I also assisted Willie George in the development of the TV show. We filmed over two hundred episodes of *The Gospel Bill Show*. In the eighties, the Family Channel picked up the program on the East Coast and aired it at 7:30 in the morning when kids were getting ready for school. It was broadcast nationwide on that channel, and when we would host meetings, particularly in the eastern part of the country, people would pack out the churches. Sometimes we had to do two or three services to accommodate the crowds.

The program aired everywhere and the reruns are still on Christian TV today. I went to Israel a few years ago and was staying on a kibbutz right by the Sea of Galilee. I turned on the TV one morning and to my surprise I saw my face on the screen. *Gospel Bill* was in Israel!

I acted, directed, and wrote some episodes, and was over the music for the show. I wrote and sang many songs that became kids' classics. The early eighties marked the birth of music videos on MTV. We were one of the first Christian ministries to do music videos, which became a popular part of the program. Songs like "Faith," "Celebrate Jesus," "Fear Not," "Sit Down Stand Up," "Bold Song," and "Inspiration" became standards at the time.

Only God knows the true numbers, but we estimate millions of children heard the gospel through the show. As I travel to churches all over America I constantly meet adults who watched the show as kids. Many tell me stories of how the Holy Spirit spoke to them through the songs they learned. I hear stories of children who were saved and healed through the lessons we taught.

I got a letter just a few years ago. The address was handwritten and the envelope felt heavy. I thought it had some coins in it, and I figured a little child had seen the show and was sending an offering. But when I opened the letter, a US Navy medallion rolled out.

It was from a young lady who was serving in the navy. The letter read, "I am twenty-one years old and I am serving my country. I was raised in a single-parent home by my mother. My mom was an atheist and told my little brother and me that we were forbidden from watching Christian TV because she said it would mess with our minds. One day when I was flipping channels I found *The Gospel Bill Show,* and my little brother and I watched it and liked it. We would get up early in the morning and watch it when my mom was asleep so she wouldn't know about it.

"One day we were watching, and at the end of the show you led a prayer for us to ask Jesus into our heart. My brother and I prayed with you and got saved that day. We are both in the navy now serving our country. This medallion represents my honor to you for the impact you've had in my life. Thank you and God bless you for your ministry."

The devil won't even wait until a child is born to begin his diabolical attack against him, but most adults totally underestimate what Jesus can do in the life of a child. The basic values that shape a person's life are determined by what he learns as a child. An International Bible Society survey indicated that 83 percent of all Christians made decisions to follow Christ between the ages of four and fourteen.[5] A later Barna Group study found that 64 percent of those surveyed accepted Christ before the age of eighteen, but only 13 percent came to Christ as an adult.[6] Although most of the churches' evangelistic efforts are geared to adults, childhood is really when a person's heart is the most tender.

Let me illustrate. When I was growing up my mother was a Christian and took me to church, but my father was not a believer, though later in life he did get saved. My maternal grandparents were committed Christians, and I can remember my grandmother reading me Bible stories from the time I was a little boy. She had a big coffee table Bible that she would open up, put on our laps, and read to me as I sat by her on the sofa. I can remember being fascinated by many of the pictures as she read the classic Bible stories.

Now, remember my story of the time Trudi was praying for me and I was running from God? If you recall I was driving down a desolate highway in the Texas panhandle. I told you how the love of God filled my car that day in a way I'll never forget. But there is another part of that story I want to share with you now.

As I was driving that day, a childhood memory came back to me. I was eleven years old and I was sitting in a class at church with five or six other boys my age. The teacher was a farmer, and his lesson that Sunday morning had something to do with prayer.

I recalled him saying, "Boys, prayer is simply talking to God. You don't have to be at church to talk to God because God is everywhere. Sometimes I talk to God when I'm driving my pickup truck. Sometimes I talk to God when I'm on my tractor plowing. God is always there with you, no matter what you're going through. If you have a need, talk to God and ask Him to help you."

Out of nowhere, that story came back to me that day in the car. As I recalled it, I heard Jesus say to me, "I'm here with you now. Why don't you call to Me? Why don't you ask Me to help you?" Even in the middle of my confusion, I sensed His love and acceptance so strongly.

But think about how God did that. A thought came back to

me from the past. I remembered something that happened to me as a child. Jesus said:

> But the Helper, the Holy Spirit, whom the Father will send in My name, He will teach you all things, and bring to your remembrance all things that I said to you.
>
> —John 14:26

Notice the verse says the Holy Spirit will teach you and bring things to your *remembrance*. You can't remember something if it has not been deposited in your memory. That is why children need to learn about Jesus and His Word at a young age. It gives the Holy Spirit something to work with when He ministers to their hearts.

This memory helped open my eyes and bring me back to God. What if that farmer hadn't taught that class that morning? Looking back, I wonder why he was teaching that class in the first place. It certainly wasn't because he wanted to get rich and famous. You don't teach children for those reasons. He probably just wanted to do something to make a difference in the lives of little boys.

That's the thing about kids. You never know what the Holy Spirit is doing in their lives. I have preached to adults and I've preached to children. Many times after preaching I have had adults come up to me and tell me how they enjoyed my message. They'll say, "That was really good, Brother Ken," or, "Today that message really helped me in this area, Brother Ken."

In all my years of preaching to thousands of little kids, I have never had a child tell me that. They never say, "Wow, your preaching changed my life today, Nicodemus." In fact, most of the time they sit there with a blank stare. I have wondered if they were getting anything I was saying. You never know what kids are thinking or how much they are listening, because often they don't respond. You can't go by what you see.

The man who taught the class that day still lives in the part of the country where I grew up. A few years ago I was visiting my parents back home and saw him in a restaurant. I shared that story with him. He got big tears in his eyes as I told him and he said, "I didn't even think you boys were listening." When you think about it, his faithfulness to do what some would see as a very small thing—teaching a class of eleven-year-old boys the gospel—affected the world. In heaven he will be rewarded for being a huge part of my ministry.

This is why I believe so strongly and preach with such passion about the importance of reaching children. I have seen its impact firsthand. I know the devil wants to keep these truths veiled. He fears the day we, the church and parents, wake up and see how important it is that our children be reached and trained for Christ.

The devil is always after the seed. He wants to keep them away from the truth of the gospel. He want adults to think they don't understand, because the devil knows children are not just a part of God's plan, they are the reason for God's plan. Children hold a very important place in God's purposes.

Priority one

The devil hates it when people get saved. When people believe the story of the Cross and receive Christ, they no longer belong to him. They belong to God and are on the road to heaven, and there is nothing he can do about it. He has to concede that. So he figures if he can't have you, he'll take your legacy. He'll destroy the next generation by keeping them from the truth. The devil is always after the seed.

This is illustrated in the story of Moses. The people in Israel were living in slavery in the land of Egypt. They cried out to

God, and He sent Moses to be their deliverer. But Pharaoh was resistant. He was like the devil. He didn't want to release the people from bondage.

So God put pressure on him by sending ten plagues. You may remember the story or the movie starring Charlton Heston. The plagues began to devastate the land of Egypt. The waters of the Nile River became blood, frogs covered the land and filled the houses, dust turned into lice, flies swarmed, all cattle and livestock died, boils and sores broke out on the Egyptians, and devastating hail combined with thunder and lightning destroyed the crops.

After all this happened, Moses told Pharaoh the next plague would be swarms of locusts. The devastation of the plagues had been incredible. Pharaoh had witnessed so much that his will was beginning to break. He told Moses, "OK. I will let you go and worship the Lord. But tell me, exactly who is going?"

Moses answered, "Everybody—our young and old, our sons and daughters, and our flocks and herds."

Look at Pharaoh's answer:

> "The LORD will certainly need to be with you if I let you take your little ones! I can see through your evil plan. Never! Only the men may go and worship the LORD, since that is what you requested." And Pharaoh threw them out of the palace.
>
> —EXODUS 10:10–11, NLT

Some believe that when Pharaoh said he would allow the men to go, he was agreeing to free the male Hebrews aged twenty to sixty.[7] That age group represented the strength of the nation at that time. But Pharaoh was very shrewd in his proposal.

If these men had gone, yes, they would have been free. But without the women and children they would have finally died out in the wilderness. And without the older people, they would not have had the wisdom they needed to move forward.

Pharaoh was willing to concede the present, but he wanted to cut off Israel's past and future. His strategy was compromise. The devil still works that way today. He may concede you coming to Christ, but he wants your kids. Our children represent our future. I am convinced most people, Christians included, are very short-sighted. They don't look very far down the road and make plans. Without vision we have no future. Our children are our future. They are our legacy. They need to know the same God who set us free.

Fast-forward forty years. The children of Israel had wandered in the wilderness for four decades, and it was finally time for them to enter the Promised Land. Moses was old and about to hand over leadership to the next generation. He exhorted them to remember what God had done and to make sure their priorities were aligned properly. New day, new time, he told them. *Focus!*

> These are the commands, decrees, and regulations that the LORD your God commanded me to teach you. You must obey them in the land you are about to enter and occupy, and you and your children and grandchildren must fear the LORD your God as long as you live. If you obey all his decrees and commands, you will enjoy a long life. Listen closely, Israel, and be careful to obey. Then all will go well with you, and you will have many children in the land flowing with milk and honey, just as the LORD, the God of your ancestors, promised you. Listen, O Israel! The LORD is our God, the LORD alone. And you must love the LORD your God with all your heart, all your soul, and all your strength. And

> you must commit yourselves wholeheartedly to these commands that I am giving you today.
>
> —Deuteronomy 6:1–6, nlt

Moses was simply saying, "Remember to keep God number one. Love Him and serve Him with all that you have. Keep God on the throne of your heart. Do what the Word says to do. This is priority number one. After that, Moses said:

> Repeat them [God's commands] again and again to your children. Talk about them when you are at home and when you are on the road, when you are going to bed and when you are getting up.
>
> —Deuteronomy 6:7, nlt

The next priority was the children. This is very simple, but it is the way life is supposed to work. This message was not only for the Jewish people; it is also for Christians living today. This is *the* vision for every marriage and family. Break it down and here's what you get:

1. Serve God with all your heart.
2. Train your children and grandchildren to love and honor God.

And notice how we are to do it. The Scripture doesn't tell us to put them in school and let the experts teach them the things of God. I'm not against Bible clubs, Sunday schools, and youth groups. But the examples we read in Scripture tell us, the parents and grandparents, to live out our faith at home and in the real world. Talk about God when your children wake up, when they go to bed, when you are driving them to school. We are supposed to make training our children in the things of God the biggest priority of our lives.

That means on your to-do list this comes before your job, ministry, hobbies, favorite football team, Facebook, Twitter, Instagram, pickup truck, and even mama. Live by God's Word and train your children to live by God's Word. This is simple yet profound. Yes, it will cost you something. No, it is not always convenient. But there is blessing from heaven associated with it. Look at what it will produce in your life:

> The LORD your God will soon bring you into the land he swore to give you when he made a vow to your ancestors Abraham, Isaac, and Jacob. It is a land with large, prosperous cities that you did not build. The houses will be richly stocked with goods you did not produce. You will draw water from cisterns you did not dig, and you will eat from vineyards and olive trees you did not plant. When you have eaten your fill in this land...
>
> —DEUTERONOMY 6:10–11, NLT

God tells us the result of serving Him with all our hearts and training our children will be that His blessing will come on our lives. And we are talking supernatural blessing here. God says He will give you cities you didn't build and houses stocked with good things you didn't purchase, and you will draw water from cisterns that you didn't dig. You will eat from vineyards and olive trees that you didn't plant. You will live a rich, fruitful, full life of blessing. This is God's will for every family. But you must qualify for it. How? You must live for God and teach your children to do the same. God loves us and wants to bless us, but if we are to walk in His abundance, we have to do it His way.

These verses in Deuteronomy 6 are some of the most important scriptures in the Bible for Jewish people. God established these commands thousands of years ago, and they are still observed today. They are called the *Shema*, and they outline the way the Jewish people are to conduct life.

A practicing Jew today wakes up in the morning and prays this passage of Scripture to begin the day. Then at night before he goes to sleep he recites this passage again. These verses begin and end the day. If it's possible, they want these verses to be the last words they say as they die. This is to be *the* guiding principle they are to live by.

The Scripture says, "You shall write them on the doorposts of your house and on your gates" (Deut. 6:9). To fulfill this verse the Jews make a small scroll, or *mezuzah*, with the words of the *Shema* written on it. The parchment is prepared by a qualified scholar who has undergone many years of meticulous training. It must be written with a quill pen in black indelible ink.

The *mezuzah* is then placed in a decorative case and affixed to the upper right corner of the doorframes of different structures and buildings. They are placed above the doors of exterior and interior walls. I have been to Israel and everywhere you go—houses, stores, restaurants, even the Knesset government building—you will find these *mezuzahs* on the doorposts.

When Jewish people who are observant enter a building or room with a *mezuzah* over the door, they will kiss their hand and reach up and touch the *mezuzah*. This is to fulfill this commandment. They practice this daily, many times a day. This truth is ever before them to remind them of how life is to be lived.

We are not Jews. We are the church of the Lord Jesus Christ. We are not commanded to make a *mezuzah* and put it on our doorposts. But the principle is true for us today. God doesn't change the way He thinks. As Christians we need to put Jesus on the throne of our heart daily, and we should constantly talk about Jesus with our children and grandchildren. God said, "I am the Lord, I change not" (Mal. 3:6, kjv).

Children were important to God in ancient history and they are important to Him today. I am hammering this point because I want you to see that this was a theme in the Bible. I want you to see the place it holds in the mind of God.

The first step in devil-proofing your children is realizing that the enemy isn't going to wait until they've grown up to begin his attack. It's not too soon to begin teaching them about Christ. Declare by faith that God's purpose for their life will be fulfilled.

In the following chapters we will look at some principles for building your house, along with practical ways you can train your children to follow God and serve Him. So let's get started.

Chapter 8

GOD CARES ABOUT CHILDREN

JESUS CAME TO earth for a clear purpose. He came to reveal the Father. He came to blow up religion and the religious ideas of the day. And in the Book of Mark Jesus confronted the traditional thinking about children:

> They brought young children to Him, that He might touch them. But the disciples rebuked those who brought them. But when Jesus saw it, He was very displeased and said to them, "Allow the little children to come to Me, and do not forbid them, for of such is the kingdom of God. Truly I say to you, whoever does not receive the kingdom of God as a little child shall not enter it." And He took them up in His arms, put His hands on them, and blessed them.
>
> —MARK 10:13–16, MEV

I want you to get the picture. People were bringing their children to Jesus. We don't know how many, but I'm guessing there was a long line. It says that Jesus was touching these children. Jesus was famous by this time for healing the sick and doing great miracles. So any mother with an ailing baby or child was probably there that day. And I'm sure children were being physically healed.

I believe Jesus was praying for these children, touching them, and imparting blessing to them. But His disciples, insightful men that they were, stepped in to try to "help." Scripture says they began to scold the crowd. "Listen people, you're going to have to break it up here. Please take your children and leave. Jesus is a very busy man. This afternoon He is preaching on the Beatitudes on the Sea of Galilee, then tonight we have a healing rally in the synagogue. Jesus is a big-time preacher. He doesn't have time to mess with these little kids."

What was Jesus's response to His disciples? It says He was "greatly displeased." That actually means He got angry. Another translation says He was indignant. That means Jesus was exasperated, disgruntled, furious, livid, irate, fuming, boiling, peeved, seeing red! He was expressing displeasure because something was *unjust*!

Sometimes we don't think about Jesus getting angry. But Jesus got angry with His disciples when they didn't discern the importance God places on children. One of the reasons He got so angry was because He had just preached to them about children in the previous chapter, and they obviously didn't get it.

I have preached about the importance of children to God's kingdom for over thirty years. And I'll be honest with you, I have walked away from meetings after preaching on this and thought to myself, "I'm not sure I communicated that clearly enough. Lord, I'm sorry. I'm not sure the people totally received it. Please help me be a better preacher."

One day I had finished preaching at a church and I was thinking, "Lord, I'm not sure these people got it." Then He clearly spoke to me and said, "Yeah, I had the same problem." I remembered this event in Mark 10 and understood what He was telling me.

My point is simply this: Jesus wants to touch children. He wants to spiritually impact a person when they are young. But children must be *brought* to Him by disciples, or we could say the adult authority in their lives. Jesus loves children, but there is no record of Him ever organizing a crusade just for children.

He didn't go door-to-door through the streets of Jerusalem asking parents if He could take their children to an event to minister to them. No. People *brought* their children to Him. Children must be brought to Jesus. Adults are responsible to create an atmosphere where Jesus can touch them.

Jesus honors the authority of adults to bring children to Him. He doesn't skirt the very authority He established. God works through the systems of authority and will not usurp them. When it comes to Jesus ministering to children, there are two primary channels of authority He honors and uses: parents and the church.

In the culture of the Jews there were two places where children were trained in the things of God: the synagogue and the home. They worked hand-in-hand in training children. In our day that would translate to the church and the home. Let's talk about how these two work together.

Training Our Children at Church

The church is the vehicle God uses to carry out His plan on the earth. The church is more than a place we go to on Sunday. The church is the body of Christ, God's people empowered by the Holy Spirit to carry out God's plan. Jesus is the head of the church, and He has appointed different people to under shepherd His church on the earth.

> Now these are the gifts Christ gave to the church: the apostles, the prophets, the evangelists, and the pastors and teachers. Their responsibility is to equip God's people to do his work and build up the church, the body of Christ.
>
> —Ephesians 4:11–12, nlt

There are five different gifts that God instituted to administrate the church: the apostle, prophet, evangelist, pastor, and teacher. When it comes to the local church, God calls pastors to lead a specific congregation. The pastor's gift is twofold: he is to lead and feed the church. In the New Testament this partnership is likened to a shepherd caring for a flock of sheep. Jesus gives us insight into how this is supposed to work in John 21.

Let me give you some backstory. In John 21 Jesus had been raised from the dead but had not ascended to heaven yet. He had appeared to His disciples before on two different occasions. One morning after some of the disciples had been fishing all night Jesus showed up bodily for the third time and was cooking breakfast for them on the seashore. Remember, we are dealing with how Jesus uses the church to minister to children.

After the disciples arrived on the shore, Jesus began a dialogue with Peter and asked him some important questions:

> So when they had eaten breakfast, Jesus said to Simon Peter, "Simon, son of Jonah, do you love Me more than these?" He said to Him, "Yes, Lord; You know that I love You." He said to him, "Feed My lambs."
>
> —JOHN 21:15, NKJV

In essence Jesus was giving Peter his personal ministry calling. He was telling Peter he was supposed to feed sheep. Peter was an apostle, but he also operated as a pastor, or a shepherd to the flock.

Two more times Jesus asked him this question, but each time it was communicated a little differently. The second time Jesus told him to feed His *sheep* (not lambs; we will come back to that). The word *feed* in verse 16 means to tend or watch over. This is talking about caring for the sheep.

The third time Jesus told him to feed His sheep (John 21:17).

The word translated feed this time means "to eat." This is referring to what sheep are to be fed—the Word of God. Jesus said, "People do not live by bread alone, but by every word that comes from the mouth of God" (NLT). Pastors feed people by giving them the anointed Word of God on an ongoing basis.

But let's go back to the first time Jesus asked Peter to feed His sheep. There are two very critical things we see here about the responsibility a pastor has toward children.

First Jesus asked Peter, "Do you love Me?" Jesus asked him this three times. The Bible says Peter became grieved because Jesus kept asking him this question, but this question preceded Jesus telling Peter about his calling. So what was Jesus trying to get Peter to see?

Pastors don't just help people in ministry because we love them. Loving people is important, but the most important reason we do ministry is because we love Jesus. We must put Jesus first. When we love Jesus first, we will ask Him what to do and do what He tells us. That is the best way to help people. Jesus loves all people, including children, and knows *exactly* how to meet their needs. The sheep aren't ours as ministers; they belong to Jesus. We feed and care for them under His leadership. He is the great shepherd and knows exactly how to care for sheep. When we follow what Jesus tells us to do to take care of sheep we will be supernaturally empowered to meet their needs.

Second Jesus told Peter three times that he was called to "feed" the sheep. The first time Jesus tells him, "Feed My lambs." The other two times Jesus says, "Feed My sheep." Why did He use "lambs" the first time? Now, get ready for some heavy revelation. Do you know what lambs are? They are baby sheep. A little, immature baby lamb is like a child. The revelation is this: Jesus called Peter to be a shepherd to *all* the sheep. Every age group. Not just the adults, but everybody, young *and* old. In fact, Jesus told Peter to feed the lambs, or children, first.

Let's look at another example of Jesus's teaching about children. Remember the parable of the sower in Matthew 13? Jesus told us understanding that parable is the key to understanding all the parables. The sower, or the farmer, is the one who plants the seed. The seed is the Word of God. The seed is life-producing, and when it is sown properly it multiplies and yields a harvest. But the seed will not produce unless it is planted. It must be put into the ground.

The ground is the human heart. But the condition of the ground, or the heart, is critical to the seed's production. The seed of God's Word is perfect and will always produce. There is no question about whether the seed is good. The productivity of the seed is determined *entirely* by the condition of the heart.

Mark 4 lists four different kinds of soil, or four conditions of the heart.

1. The wayside, or ground (a heart) that is hard like a road. This is a person who hears the Word of God but allows the birds (birds represent the devil and demons) to immediately talk them out of believing the truth they heard.
2. Stony ground. This is someone who hears the truth and gets excited initially, but because their heart is hard they look at their circumstances and say, "This is too good to be true," and they reject the truth.
3. Thorny ground, or ground that is overrun by weeds. This represents someone who allows sin and worldly pursuits to dominate their thinking to the point that the Word is choked out.
4. Good ground. This is someone who hears the Word and believes it. This is a person who

> doesn't spend his time listening to Satan, but has a tender heart and is not dominated by the distractions of life. This is pure, untapped, fertile, productive soil.

The good ground is productive. Seed sown there will produce an abundant harvest. This is the perfect picture of the heart of a child. Children are like a blank slate. Children are innocent and inexperienced. They will quickly believe what you tell them. When my kids were young, sometimes we would be driving down the road and I might say, "Look up there. There is an elephant sitting in that tree!" Every time I would do that they would look out the window, fully expecting to see an elephant sitting on a tree branch.

Adults wouldn't buy that. Their experience tells them elephants can't climb trees and even if they could, they are too heavy for a tree's branches to hold them. But not children. They believe what you tell them. They have no cynicism yet. Their hearts are pure and fertile and looking for something to believe. They are like a blank canvas waiting to be painted on. This is the best time to put the seed of God's Word into their little hearts.

So children are like little lambs. They have pure hearts that are wide open to eat the Word of God. Pastors in local churches are called to lead and feed every age group, from those who are in their nineties to the infants in the nursery. But different age groups need to be fed differently. Adults like to eat steak, but you can't feed steak to the babies in the nursery. They would choke. You have to feed them milk until they grow. That is why many churches have the different age groups meet in different places. It's so each group can receive teaching on their level.

David was a shepherd. The reason he was such a great king is because he was such a skilled shepherd. He knew how to care for sheep. Ancient Jewish wisdom says that David fed the sheep according to what they needed for their different ages. He would feed the older sheep the roots of the grass because it contained nutrients they needed at their age. He fed the mature sheep the stalk of the grass, because he knew they would be able to chew it properly and have their needs met. But he gave the lambs only the top part of the grass, the flowering part, because it was tender and easier for them to chew.[1]

Good pastors realize they need to feed the Word of God differently to the differing age groups in the church. Ministry to children is one of the most important ministries in the church. It is more than childcare so the adults can listen to the sermon without distraction. It is legitimate ministry and must be respected as such.

TRAINING OUR CHILDREN AT HOME

As much as we all need a pastor and a local church that we are committed to and involved in, God didn't give our children to the church. Our children don't belong to the government either. God gives children to families—a man and a woman who commit to each other for a lifetime and promise to nurture and protect their children. God expects parents to train their own children. The church is designed to reinforce what children are learning about God at home; it should not be the only source of a child's spiritual training.

As parents, the most important thing we can teach our children is to know Jesus and believe His Word. Remember, the devil is always after the seed. His desire is to exert his influence on a person's life from a young age, and he is serious and ruthless in his pursuit. He wants to pervert people's minds in their youth by subverting their spiritual training.

The devil's cold-blooded tactics can be revealed in the life of Josef Stalin, the Russian dictator. In his book *Can Man Live*

Without God, Ravi Zacharias writes about the treachery of Stalin, who masterminded the large-scale murder of his own people. As many as fifteen million people lost their lives because of his actions. The irony of this is he was being trained for ministry and had gone to seminary. But as a young man, somewhere in his formative years, he learned something that caused him to break away from God. He became a God-hater.

The story is told that one day Stalin gathered his top leaders and used this illustration to make an unforgettable point to them. He called for a live chicken and had his henchmen watch as he systematically plucked the feathers, one by one, from the struggling, terrified bird. He continued until the bird was completely stripped.

Then he put the terror-stricken chicken down on the floor and said, "Now, watch this." He walked away and with each step dropped some bread crumbs he had in his hand. Astonishingly, the bird began to follow him as he walked around the room. Stalin told his leaders, "This is the way to rule people. Did you see how that chicken followed me for food, even though I had caused it such torture? People are like that chicken. If you inflict inordinate pain on them, they will follow you for food for the rest of their lives."[2]

Stalin's daughter tells the story that on his deathbed he was tormented by horrible hallucinations. Yet she said right before he took his last breath, he raised up in bed, looked toward heaven, and angrily shook his fist toward God.[3]

We don't know exactly what happened to warp this man's mind, but some ideology was conceived that took him in the direction of conquest and murder. And it happened when he was young and impressionable.

In the death camps of Auschwitz and Birkenau, the words of Adolf Hitler hung on the wall, "I freed Germany from the stupid and degrading fallacies of conscience and morality... We will train young people before whom the world will tremble. I want young people capable of violence—imperious, relentless and cruel."[4]

Satan is serious about getting his hooks into a person's life. He knows the ideal time to do it is when they are young. I'm not saying if parents don't train their children in the things of God their children will grow up to be like Hitler or Stalin. But I do want us to see the seriousness of training our children. They will become what is deposited in them, and the primary trainers and influencers of their lives, as designed by God, are the parents. We must take this training seriously. In the next two chapters, we will look at specific ways parents can train their children so the enemy can't easily get his hooks into them.

Chapter 9

A BLUEPRINT FOR BUILDING STRONG FAMILIES

THE BIBLE OFFERS what I like to think of as a blueprint for building a strong family. These principles are found in Psalm 127.

> Unless the LORD builds the house, they labor in vain who build it; unless the LORD guards the city, the watchman stays awake in vain. It is vain for you to rise up early, to sit up late, to eat the bread of sorrows; for so He gives His beloved sleep. Behold, children are a heritage from the LORD, the fruit of the womb is a reward. Like arrows in the hand of a warrior, so are the children of one's youth. Happy is the man who has his quiver full of them; they shall not be ashamed, but shall speak with their enemies in the gate.

This short, five-verse psalm contains tremendous insight into parenting. In fact, Jewish rabbis teach that this psalm contains the pattern for training children to serve God. Remember, when we see the word *house* in Scripture we can often substitute the word *family*. So in this chapter we are going to look closely at the wisdom found in Psalm 127 for building a family that serves God and stands firm against the enemy.

1. Be committed

The psalm begins by telling us that unless we build the house God's way, our effort is in vain. The word "vain" is used three times in the first two verses of this psalm. Do you think God is trying to get something across to us? If we try to raise our children without Him, we are in trouble, because our efforts will be in vain.

It is possible to work hard to build something and have that work produce nothing. That's what it means to labor in vain. The effort is useless. It will not produce fruit or longevity. God's way is the way of blessing. It will produce fruit in the long run. But it is not always the easy way.

When you commit to live by God's Word, you are bucking the trends of the world in which we live. The world tells us there are many paths to God, if He even exists, but we know there is only one God and only one mediator between Him and mankind, and His name is Jesus (1 Tim. 2:5). The world tells us there is no such thing as absolute truth, but Scripture says God's Word is truth (John 17:17). It's not merely "true"; it's *the truth.*

When you are living by God's Word, you are swimming upstream, and it will not be easy. Sometimes it may even look like living according to God's Word is not working. But if you want to protect your children from the enemy's traps, the most important thing you can do is make a determined commitment to live God's way and not waver.

There are many voices crying out to our children—the ones on TV and in the media, the ones at school, the ones from their friends, and the ones on social media—and those voices are not always easy to resist. The only way you can teach your children to follow God's ways when it seems everyone around them is doing the opposite is if you are unequivocal and unyielding in your commitment to follow God. The devil is unflinching in his determination to teach your children his lies, and you have to be just as steadfast in your stand for Christ. You have to be tough!

2. Rely on the Holy Spirit

It is impossible to have this kind of resolve on your own. But the good news is, you don't have to do it alone! If you will make the commitment to serve God wholeheartedly, He will help you live out that commitment.

Notice Psalm 127:1 says, "unless the Lord build the house..." and "unless the Lord guards the city..." This indicates that we must have God's help. God has given us His Word as the blueprint for training our children, but He also has given us a living Helper to guide and counsel us in the process. He is the Holy Spirit! If you are going to build a family who loves and follows God, you *must* learn to hear the voice of the Holy Spirit.

Jesus said, "And I will pray the Father, and He will give you another Helper, that He may abide with you forever—the Spirit of truth, whom the world cannot receive, because it neither sees Him nor knows Him; but you know Him, for He dwells with you and will be in you" (John 14:16–17).

The Bible is our guidebook for raising kids. It is the truth that never changes, even in the face of cultural change. We must be steadfast students of God's Word to build our family on the proper foundation. What do I mean by that? You need to attend a church where God's Word is taught uncompromisingly. Read the Scriptures for yourself (everyone needs a daily Bible reading program), find good Christian books, and listen to solid Bible teachers regularly so you can grow spiritually. The good news is that in this digital age there are more good resources available now than ever.

When you base your beliefs on God's Word, you will know the Lord's voice. God uses these two witnesses—His voice and

His Word—to supernaturally guide you to success. Let me illustrate what I mean.

Trudi and I had been married for about three years when she was diagnosed with endometriosis. Her doctor said the only way to relieve the pain she was experiencing and cure this disease was for her to have a hysterectomy. That, of course, would mean we wouldn't be able to have children.

We didn't know what to do. We sought counsel from our church. One of the pastors told us, "It could be the will of God for you to never have children. Sometimes God uses things like this to teach you lessons." This was very discouraging counsel for a very discouraging situation, because we had a strong desire to have children.

We were holding off on the hysterectomy, still waiting for God to tell us what to do. Then one day Trudi was just minding her own business, reading the Bible, when she came across this scripture:

> He maketh the barren woman to keep house, and to be a joyful mother of children. Praise ye the LORD.
>
> —PSALM 113:9, KJV

When Trudi read that verse, the words seemed to explode in her spirit. The Holy Spirit made those words come alive in her. She began to think, "God makes the barren woman to be a mother. The will of God is His Word. The will of God is not for me to be barren. The will of God is for me to have children. Those people who told me barrenness is the will of God must have never read this scripture." She received God's Word with childlike faith.

When I came home, she shared with me what she had read. We prayed together with confidence and began to claim this scripture that the Holy Spirit had shown her. It was during this time that her sister gave her a dress that her own baby had worn and told her, "One day your little baby girl will wear this dress."

She kept that dress with her in the house all the time. If she was cooking in the kitchen, she would have the dress on the counter. When we were watching TV, she would hold the dress. Every night when we went to bed she would sleep with the dress. We didn't realize it at the time, but the Holy Spirit was leading her to do this. He was using that dress to build faith on the inside of her.

This went on for about six months. Then one day at one of her regular appointments, the doctor came and said, "Mrs. Blount, we have no way to explain what has happened, but you are pregnant!" I'll never forget when she called me and told me the news. We were ecstatic.

But remember, the devil is always after the seed. Trudi was six weeks from delivering the baby when she began to have discomfort and swelling in her legs. When we went to the doctor they discovered her blood pressure was at a dangerously high level. She had developed toxemia, also known as preeclampsia, and they needed to do an emergency C-section.

This was in 1975, and technology was not the same then. A C-section was major surgery. They didn't know if the baby would be mature enough to live, but Trudi's condition demanded the surgery. Her kidneys were beginning to shut down, so both of their lives were on the line.

The delivery was scheduled for early morning. The night before, some Christian friends came to see her. They were well-meaning, but they tried to prepare her for the worst. They told her, "It might not be God's will for this baby to live." They didn't want her to be disappointed.

That night when everyone left she lay in the hospital bed alone, pondering what had been said. Out of nowhere she remembered an old hymn she had heard growing up in church. It goes like this:

> Shut in with God in a secret place.
> Here in His presence, beholding His face
> Gaining new power to run in this race
> I long to be shut in with God.[1]

I'll let Trudi tell you what happened next: "As I lay there I began to sing out the words to that song. As I sang it, I sensed the presence of God come into the room. I shut my eyes, and I sensed the presence of the Holy Spirit so strong, I was afraid to open them. I was afraid I would see Jesus standing before me! It felt like the Lord put His hands on my abdomen, and I heard these words: 'I am the life giver. No matter how old or how young, I'm the one who gives life.' After I heard that, I knew that I knew that the baby and I would be fine. I felt perfect peace. I closed my eyes and went to sleep."

The next morning at 11:31, our little baby girl was born. She weighed four pounds, two ounces. She was very small, but she was perfect, and her mother was fine. I spoke with the doctor after the delivery, and he said, "Mr. Blount, I just want you to know that this surgery was textbook. If one little thing had gone wrong we could have lost your baby, your wife, or both."

That little baby is in her thirties now with two girls of her own. *Unless the Lord builds the house*—thank God for the power of His promise. Thank God for the help of the Holy Spirit. We are not doing this alone. We have to do our part to raise our children, but we need to make much of the Lord who is with us to help us build our house.

Make a big deal about the power of God at work in your family. Pray about the challenges you face. Pray with your kids. Let them see that as parents you are trusting in God and honoring Him in your house. Invite Jesus into your house daily. (At the end of this book, we have included a prayer for families that you can use to jump-start your prayer time.) He wants to live there but He must be welcomed in. No matter what you are facing in your family. No matter how young your children may be, no matter how old, nothing is impossible with God.

3. Partner with your spouse

Let's look again at Psalm 127:1: "Unless the LORD builds the house, they labor in vain who build it; unless the LORD guards the city, the watchman stays awake in vain." According to ancient Jewish wisdom, the builder here represents the father in the family, and the watchman represents the mother.[2] The husband is the one who leads in constructing the house, but the wife is the watcher. This goes along with what we taught earlier about the way women see details men don't naturally spot.

By God's design the father and mother have separate and distinct roles to help build the family. But the mother and father are to bring their unique strengths together and work as a team to train their children. As parents, your agreement is very important because kids will try to "divide and conquer." Make it clear that you will not allow this kind of behavior. If you don't agree with the way your spouse is handling something, don't argue about it in front of your children. Go behind closed doors and discuss the situation until you come to a unified decision.

You may be wondering what happens in single-parent homes. How can a single parent partner with his or her spouse? Of course, single parents face some special challenges. But I have some good news. God offers unique help for single parents.

> Fear not; you will no longer live in shame. Don't be afraid; there is no more disgrace for you. You will no longer remember the shame of your youth and the sorrows of widowhood. For your Creator will be your

> husband; the LORD of Heaven's Armies is his name! He is your Redeemer, the Holy One of Israel, the God of all the earth.
>
> —ISAIAH 54:4–5, NLT

God promises that if you are raising children alone, if you will trust in Him, walk closely with Him, and rely on the Holy Spirit's guidance, He will lead you in raising godly children. His presence will be your absent spouse. There is great healing and strength in these verses from Isaiah, and we encourage you to pray and meditate on them if you are a single parent.

If you are raising children alone, the local church is also a very important resource. Being involved in a good local church will allow your children to observe men and women serving Jesus and provide much needed role models for them. God is for you, and as you seek Him, He will provide what you need to raise children who buck the negative societal trends.

Yes, there will be challenges in parenting whether you are married or single. But the Holy Spirit is ever-present to give you wisdom. He can and will lead you through the most difficult circumstances, if you will ask Him.

4. Give your worries to the Lord

Psalm 127:2 tells us, "It is vain for you to rise up early, to sit up late, to eat the bread of sorrows; for so He gives His beloved sleep." What is God saying here? What is all this about staying up late, getting up early, and eating the bread of sorrows? This sounds like somebody who is burdened with worry.

I believe God is letting us know that things will not always go perfectly in parenting (if you think they will, you are not living in the real world). But if we cast our cares upon the Lord, He will fill our hearts with peace.

I remember how idealistic Trudi and I were when we had our first baby. We wanted to be the perfect parents. We loved Jesus and just knew we were going to raise the perfect child. We were naive and had a lot to learn.

Yes, children can meet Jesus when they are young and be trained in the Word of God (we will explain how to do this in chapter 11), but that doesn't mean they will be perfect. They are human beings just like me and you. They are subject to the Fall. They will make mistakes—and so will you. As a parent you will miss it sometimes, and sorrow may come on you when you do.

In Psalm 127 God is trying to let you know that challenges *will* come. And when they do, you have to learn to believe that the Lord will show you how to deal with the situation. He will meet you right where you are.

Most parents, even great parents, have regrets about the way they trained their children. I have my own regrets. I made parenting mistakes. But I knew I could never just throw up my hands and quit. None of us can. We have to trust that God will help us even in the middle of a mess we've made.

I want to encourage you right now to let go of any guilt you may have over parenting blunders. You may need to ask God to forgive you because you haven't been the kind of father or mother you know you should have been. You may need to go to your children and admit to them you missed it and ask them to forgive you. I've done that myself more than once. You may need to forgive them because of how they hurt you.

Wherever you may be as a parent it's time to move on. Let go of the sorrow and regret. Give the worry to Jesus. The Bible says:

> So humble yourselves under the mighty power of God, and at the right time he will lift you up in honor. Give all your worries and cares to God, for he cares about you. Stay alert! Watch out for your great enemy, the

> devil. He prowls around like a roaring lion, looking for someone to devour.
>
> —1 PETER 5:6–8, NLT

There it is again. It is the devil that wants to keep you in bondage to past mistakes and sin. It is time for you to give your sorrows to God. Let them go and move into your future. Pray this prayer with me, out loud if you can:

> *Heavenly Father, I come to You in Jesus's name. I humble myself under Your mighty hand right now. I do so by giving You all my worries and cares about my family and children. I receive forgiveness for the times when I have missed it as a parent. I cast all my regrets, worries, and cares on You. I receive healing from You right now. I refuse to worry about the past, and I entrust my marriage and children to You. I thank You for helping me by Your mighty power. I believe You will honor me, as 1 Peter 5:6 says. In Jesus's name, amen.*

Near the end of Psalm 127:2, there is a great promise. It declares that God gives His beloved sleep. At times you will be tempted to stay up late and worry about your children. You may wake up in the middle of the night tempted to fret about their future. But God doesn't want you to be burdened by worry. He wants to give you rest and peace. He wants you to be able to sleep through the night knowing that He is taking care of your family.

The Amplified Bible says, "He gives blessings to His beloved in sleep." I like that wording because it means God is working on your situation even when you are asleep. When you lay your cares on Him, you can put your head down on the pillow at night and have confidence that God is moving supernaturally in your family. You may be tempted to pick those worries back up. I know how the devil works. But when those anxious or sorrowful thoughts come, just remind the enemy that you trust God to take care of you and your family. Resist the devil, and he will flee from you (James 4:7)!

Be diligent to do your part, and then trust God to do what you cannot.

5. Be faithful stewards

Psalm 127:3 tells us, "Behold, children are a heritage from the LORD, the fruit of the womb is a reward." Our children are the greatest reward we can receive in this life. No matter how much money we may make, no matter what we achieve in this life, it all pales in comparison to the gift God gives us in a child. Look at the beautiful wording of Psalm 139 that describes the care God takes when He creates a human being.

> You made all the delicate, inner parts of my body and knit them together in my mother's womb. Thank you for making me so wonderfully complex! It is amazing to think about. Your workmanship is marvelous—and how well I know it. You were there while I was being formed in utter seclusion! You saw me before I was born and scheduled each day of my life before I began to breathe. Every day was recorded in your book!
>
> —PSALM 139:13–16, TLB

Our children are the only things we could ever take with us to heaven. We'll never see our houses, cars, or money again once we leave this earth. But if our children know Christ, we will be with them for eternity.

Notice Psalm 127:3 says they are the heritage of the Lord. Our children really don't belong to us. They belong to Jesus. I tweeted this recently: "Parenting is stewardship. We are caring for them and training them so that we can return them to the rightful owner, their Father God." We only lease our children for a while, but our parenting can make the difference in where they spend eternity. This is something we need to take very seriously.

The word "heritage" actually means something inherited. Children are our inheritance. Think about it this way. Let's say you had a rich uncle who left you his entire estate: three hundred acres and a large Victorian mansion with thirty-three bedrooms and twenty-four bathrooms. Inside the house are beautiful wood floors and expensive furniture in every room. Outside the grounds are well manicured, and the landscaping is perfectly trimmed. The estate even has an Olympic-size swimming pool and a duck pond. And it all has your name on it. It is your inheritance.

But the estate won't stay perfect and immaculate forever. It is going to take a lot of work, organization, manpower, and financial investment to maintain it. If this is not done, the property will quickly deteriorate.

Your children are much the same way. They have been bequeathed to you. Your name is on them, and God has given you the responsibility for their future. Like the estate in the illustration, this inheritance requires your care and investment. You have been entrusted by your heavenly Father to steward this young life. Parenting is serious business.

To be a doctor you have to go through extensive training. Doctors hold people's lives in their hands, and our society takes that very seriously. To be an attorney you have to go through extensive study and pass the bar exam. You even have to pass a test to get a driver's license. But there are no qualifications to be a parent. There is no parenting school. You can't get a BA or PhD in parenting. Yet parents are molding the eternal soul of a human being.

Parenting is serious business. It is a set of skills you can develop as you study resources like this one. But I also believe God gives parents an anointing, or a spiritual gifting, to train and love their own children. There is a longing in children's hearts to learn from their parents. Nobody carries more weight with the words they speak than parents. In the same way, nothing can hurt like the destructive words of parents. Be an example of God's unconditional love and determine to plant God's Word into your child's heart from a young age. (We will share more about this in the next chapter.)

6. Develop a warrior mind-set

Psalm 127:4–5 says, "Like arrows in the hand of a warrior, so are the children of one's youth. Happy is the man who has his quiver full of them; they shall not be ashamed, but shall speak with their enemies in the gate." In this verse God likens children to arrows. What is an arrow? It is a weapon.

You have to come to grips with the fact that you are not training them in neutral territory. You are doing this in a war zone. This world is hostile territory. You are being actively opposed. You will be shot at.

Statistics tell us that every twenty-four hours in America:

- 2,899 babies are aborted[3]
- 2,857 students drop out of high school[4]
- 4,028 children are arrested[5]
- 4,408 babies are born to unmarried mothers[6]
- About 2,800 teens abuse prescription drugs for the first time[7]

In 1960 roughly 85 percent of children under the age of eighteen were living in two-parent homes. By 2012 that number decreased to 64 percent and continues to trend downward.[8] These statistics point to the fact that things aren't looking up in our society. They are trending downward.

We have to develop a warrior mind-set. We must be military-minded, like we're training soldiers to go to war. We have to be very deliberate in training our kids. The devil is serious about taking them down. He fires real bullets.

Psalm 127:4–5 likens our children to arrows. An arrow is designed to hurt an enemy. When our kids are trained to be arrows for God, they become an offensive weapon that will do damage to the kingdom of darkness.

But the preparation of the arrow is crucial. My son-in-law, Scott, is an avid hunter. His weapon of choice is the bow and arrow. When deer hunting season is approaching, Scott begins getting his equipment ready. He spends hours checking his bow and arrows so everything is in prime condition. He knows he can't wait until a deer is in front of him to ready his weapon.

Arrow preparation is critical. There are three parts to an arrow that must be examined. Each of these has significant application to the training of our children.

The feathers must be in good shape, with no frays or tears.

Feathers are critical because they guide the arrow to the target. Parents are like those feathers. We must provide guidance so our children will stay on the right course. Proverbs 22:6 says if we train up a child in the way he should go, when he is old he won't depart from it. This training is twofold: (1) We teach them truth based on Bible principles, and (2) we live the truth out in front of them.

Ephesians 5:1 says, "Be ye therefore followers of God, as dear children" (KJV). The word "follower" in this verse actually means imitator. Children imitate what they see. The younger they are the more they imitate. They act out the things they observe and admire. That's why you can't teach your children to live by principles that you are not modeling in front of them regularly. It just won't work. The kids see through it and will imitate what you are actually doing. None of us are perfect, but the most effective training we give our kids is the life we live before them. If you want your children to live for God, be a good guide by modeling that life of faith before them and by being intentional about teaching them God's Word.

The shaft must be straight.

The shaft of the arrow is the foundation, and if it isn't straight it will veer when fired. The shaft is like our children's relationship with God. We must lead our children to have their own relationship with the Lord so they will not always rely on ours. Proverbs 3:5–6 says if we acknowledge God in all our ways, He will make our paths straight. It is important that your children see you living for God and being sensitive to the Holy Spirit. But at some point they must acknowledge God for themselves. This is vitally important, and in chapter 11 we will discuss at length how to lead your children to Christ even at a very young age. When our children have a relationship with Christ, they will be guided by the Holy Spirit and able to resist the traps of the enemy.

The arrowhead must be sharp.

That's because it is the part that does the damage. We must train our children in the Word, because it is their weapon against the enemy. Ephesians 6 lists the full armor of God, but all of the armor is defensive except the sword of the Spirit, which is the Word of God. The Bible says the Word is "living and powerful, and sharper than any two-edged sword, piercing even to the division of soul and spirit" (Heb. 4:12). Our children will be powerless against the enemy without the knowledge of His Word. Reading the Bible to them when they are young, having family devotions as they get older, and encouraging them to study the Scriptures for answers to their questions will help them recognize and resist the lies of the enemy when they hear them passed off as political correctness. When children are guided by godly parents and taught God's Word, their faith becomes sharp, and they will be able to pierce through the darkness of the world and the lies of the enemy to fulfill their unique purpose.

This training process requires great diligence and patience. As I mentioned earlier, the Bible says, "Train up a child in the way he should go: and when he is old, he will not depart from it" (Prov. 22:6, KJV). The verse doesn't say, "*Teach* your child in the way he should go." It uses the word *train*. To train means to make proficient by instruction and practice, as in some art, profession, or work: to train soldiers.[9]

I hope you caught that military reference. We are preparing our children to be offensive weapons that do damage to the enemy, and that preparation comes through training. Training is a process. To train your children means you are living out the principles you teach along with them. It means after you give them instruction on how to do something, you show them how to do it. And when they don't do it exactly right, you come back and show them where they missed it and you go over it again.

Proverbs 22:6 also says to train *up* a child. Think about that for a minute. Up is positive. Our attitude as we train them in both spiritual and natural things is critical. As parents we have to maintain a positive attitude, even when we correct our children. It's easy to get negative and think, "I've told you this a million times. Are you never going to get this?" With that kind of attitude you could be right. They may never get it. Always train with a positive attitude.

The verse also says to train them up in the way they should go. It doesn't say to train them in the way you think they should go or the way you want them to go. It's the way *they* should go. A great part of parenting is being able to recognize the gifts God puts in your children and help them develop their own God-given talents.

Many parents try to live vicariously through their children.

They want their children to be what *they* want them to be. Maybe a father had the lofty ambition to play football but he didn't get to play in the NFL like he dreamed. Now he has a son. Dad wants him to play football and so he diligently encourages, even pushes, him to play. That could be fine if the son wants to play. But what if that is not his gift?

I am the oldest of two sons. My father was a farmer, and a very good one. As I grew up, I learned many valuable things working on the farm. I learned how to work hard. In the summer we worked twelve- to fourteen-hour days. I learned not to quit. But my little brother was the more natural farmer. He plowed better than I did and just generally loved farming more than I did. Farming has been his lifelong career.

I worked on the farm but it was not my passion. I enjoyed music and my interests were just generally different from his. My father wanted me to love farming like he did, but I just didn't enjoy it as much as my brother did.

Because of that, a wedge developed between my dad and me. He didn't know how to relate to me. He seemed to favor my little brother over me. I felt like he was disappointed in me, and at times I thought he loved my little brother more than me because their interests were more alike. As a result I developed feelings of inferiority. I dealt with a lot of insecurity growing up. Those feelings persisted into my adulthood, and it is something I still battle with at times.

But the truth is, I wasn't supposed to be a farmer. I was supposed to be in the ministry and write and record music. Those were the gifts my heavenly Father invested in me. As parents we need to be sensitive to the natural gifts God has invested in our children and help them discover who they really are supposed to be, not just what we want them to be.

When my daughter was growing up, she was a typical teenage girl. Trudi and I tried to discover what interested her. I bought her a really nice camera because for a while she showed some interest in photography, but that lasted about three days. The thing she spent the most time on was putting on makeup. It seemed like all her time was spent in the bathroom with makeup.

One day I told Trudi, "I don't know what Brooke is going to do in life. All she wants to do is put on makeup. But you can't make a living just putting on makeup." Boy was I wrong.

After she graduated she got a job as a makeup artist at Saks Fifth Avenue, the highest end department store in an exclusive mall in our city. When she first married, she was making more money than her husband and their insurance benefits came through her job. Although she quit that job and became a full-time mom, she still uses her makeup training. Her husband is a gymnastics coach and runs his own gym. When the little girls do events they allow them to wear makeup. Brooke still uses skills as a makeup artist on those young gymnasts.

As parents we need to be sensitive to direct our children to their unique interests. Ask the Holy Spirit to help you see what God put inside them.

At the end of Proverbs 22:6, the verse says, "When he is old he will not depart from it" (KJV). This tells us that if we train our children properly, following the pattern we've discussed, they won't depart from that training when they get old.

You may be thinking, "But that's not true! I know people who trained their children, and still their kids are not serving God." This verse is not saying our children will never have issues or never stray from God. The phrase "when he is old" is actually referring to old age. This is talking about somebody at the end of life. Maybe a child has turned away from God. Maybe he has been away from Him for a while. But this verse is saying the godly training he received as a child will continue to work on him.

I believe that training is like a hook on the inside of them. Our children are human. They will be tempted and maybe even give in to temptation. But the training you invest in them will continue to pull them back. It never leaves them. They may resist, but it will work on them all the days of their life.

This doesn't mean if you train them in the things of God they will never turn away from God. Everybody has a free will. God won't make anybody do anything. But He will pull on people and love them until the day they die. Training is part of the hook God will use to pull our children back if they stray.

Maybe you have children who are not serving Jesus. Maybe they were trained in the things of God but walked away from Him. Maybe you got saved later in life and didn't train your children for Christ when they were young. If that is the case, remember this awesome promise God has given us:

> Believe in the Lord Jesus and you will be saved, along with everyone in your household.
>
> —Acts 16:31, NLT

If you will claim this scripture for your kids, it will release God to work on them—and anyone else in your family. God desires that everyone be saved and come into the knowledge of the truth. Your children are no exception.

When I received Christ years ago the first person I wanted to share it with was my dad. My mom was a Christian but my dad was not. I sat across the table from him one day and shared what Jesus had done in my life. His reply was, "I don't want you to talk about this to me. I forbid you from mentioning this in my house again."

It broke my heart, but I had to obey him. I didn't mention anything about God to him, but I found this scripture and began to pray it. I prayed this word over my dad every day. One day I was mopping a floor in a little restaurant Trudi and I owned, just minding my own business, when in my spirit I heard as clear as a bell, "Your father will be saved." I knew that I knew the Lord spoke to me and that my dad would come to know Him. From that moment, I had a confidence that this would happen, and I hung on to that word.

It was nine years later when I got a call from my mom. She and my dad were on vacation, and he had gone to church with her. When they returned to the hotel room she began to talk with him about what they had heard. She asked him if he would like to receive Jesus, and he prayed with her in the hotel room.

My dad is in heaven today. It was not my preaching or pleading with him that got him saved. But my prayers played a big part. Even if you're in a place where you can't talk to your children about God, you can always pray. Claim the promise in Acts 16:31 for your family members who are away from God. Keep praying for your children and your unsaved family members. Don't give up on them. Prayer changes things.

8. It's worth it

Let's conclude with the last verse of Psalm 127.

> Happy is the man who has his quiver full of them; they shall not be ashamed, but shall speak with their enemies in the gate.

Training your children is work. Let's just be honest. That's why a lot of parents don't do it. But it is worth it. It will produce good fruit for you. If you will plant and nurture the seed of your children, in time harvest is guaranteed. Harvest time is happy time.

Psalm 127:5 tells us if we build our house God's way, we won't be ashamed. What does that mean? In Bible times, cities had walls around them. The gate was the place for city activity and community action. In the Law of Moses, parents of a rebellious son were told to bring him to the city gate, where the elders would examine the evidence and pass judgment (Deut. 21:18–21).

Before mass media and the Internet, people would gather at the gate to fellowship and speak about the issues of the day. When a person of reputation spoke, they were shown more respect. So the promise given in Psalm 127:5 is that when we as parents train our children, a day will come when they will stand in a place of prominence.

The verse also says that even their enemies would be forced to listen to them. I believe when we train our children and develop them spiritually the devil will have to shut his mouth and back off. There is a payday. It is all worth the effort.

Parents, keep your eyes on the prize. It seems like childhood lasts forever when you are in the middle of it, but life is short. Take the time to invest in your children. There is a day coming when they will humiliate the devil and his plan. When that happens, I promise it will make you very happy.

Chapter 10

RESISTING THE CULTURE

STRAP ON YOUR cowboy boots and put on your big boy pants. This is about to get a little tough. We are training our children to live in victory over the enemy. We are training them to be champions. Champions aren't average. They live differently. They prepare themselves for the battles that are ahead.

The devil is against us, and so is the culture. The culture is trying to shape our children. As parents we need to understand how to develop our children to resist the culture that wants to mold them.

There are five basic areas in which every person must develop in order to be healthy:

1. Emotional development, which determines how we handle life
2. Intellectual development, which determines how we think
3. Physical development, which determines our physical fitness
4. Moral development, which determines the moral compass that directs our decisions
5. Spiritual development, which determines the growth of our eternal spirit, the real person who lives eternally.

If we are to devil-proof our children, we must understand each of these areas and how the enemy would use them to thwart God's plans for our children's lives.

Emotional development

The key word in emotional development is acceptance. Children either grow up seeking and trying to gain acceptance, or they grow up knowing that they are accepted. The family was meant to be a nurturing place where children could grow knowing that no matter what they may do, they are loved and accepted. If they don't get this acceptance at home they will look for it from other people.

It begins around age eleven or twelve. That's when children begin to splinter into different groups because they are looking for identity and acceptance. Kids will gravitate toward the cool group, the geeks, the jocks, the Goths, and so on. They may change the way they dress and act, mostly because they are looking for an identity.

As parents we must make home the place of acceptance. This acceptance is twofold.

Our children must know that their parents love and accept them, not because of how they perform but simply because they are your children and you love them unconditionally. For instance, when they do something wrong, always separate the offense from the person. Condemn the wrong act but never the person. Show your children how to correct their mistake, but always let them know you love them no matter what—even when they do something wrong. Your children must know that your love for them will never change regardless of how they act.

Secondly they must know that God loves and accepts them. Again, they must realize God's love is not based on what they do; it is based on what Jesus did. He died in our place, and when they receive Jesus as their Savior (we will talk about leading your children to Christ in the next chapter), they have been made righteous by God—and God loves His children unconditionally.

Knowing we are loved and accepted unconditionally is the basis for successful emotional development. When your kids know their parents love and accept them unconditionally, and that God loves and accepts them unconditionally, they will have the healthy foundation of self-esteem they will need to face the negative things that will come against them in life.

Intellectual development

We want our children to develop intellectually, so we send them to school to learn, and that is important. But there are two areas of intellectual development: knowledge and wisdom. We can teach our children that they need to go to school and make good grades so they can get a good job. But that is only part of success. Knowledge is the accumulation of facts and information learned, but wisdom is different. Wisdom is the ability to wisely and practically apply the knowledge that you have gained.

If they don't get wisdom, they won't know how to handle the money they make in their careers. The basis for true financial success—and every other kind of success—is training our children to honor God first with the resources He gives them.

There are many ways wisdom must be applied in life, but I want to especially encourage you to train your children in financial stewardship from a young age. This will firmly establish the importance of honoring God with money instead of chasing material things.

When our children are young, we can begin teaching them the benefits of tithing, saving, and wise spending. This needs to start as young as age three. How? If you give your three-year-old a dollar, don't give him a dollar bill. Give him ten dimes. Tell him he can keep nine dimes but he needs to honor Jesus with one of those dimes, because He is the one who gave us all the dimes. Even at that young age, you can teach your child that when we honor Jesus with what He gives us, He will give us more.

We need to teach our children to tithe and be generous so they can live a truly blessed life. We also need to teach them the value of money and how to spend and save. They need to learn that money is for more than just downloading cool music and buying the latest video game. We want them to develop in knowledge and wisdom, and teaching our children financial stewardship is one way we do that.

Physical development

In order to fulfill your purpose in life you need a healthy physical body. Champions don't just eat anything and do anything they want with their bodies. Our children need to be taught that their bodies are the house where God lives and we have to honor God in our house.

There are two basic ways we train children in their physical development.

We teach them to eat healthily.

Most restaurants today have healthy options for adults, but offer kids pizza, macaroni and cheese, chicken fingers, and hot dogs. Children need healthy food just as much as adults, maybe more. As parents we need to make sure they are eating wholesome food. Children are ruled by their flesh, and if you let them they would most likely only eat Twinkies, ice cream, and other foods that offer little nutrition. We need to train our children to eat right so they will have a healthy body with which to honor Jesus.

We teach them that what they do with their body is important. Children today spend hours watching TV and huge amounts of time playing video games. Many parents are unaware of the violence and perversion on many of these games. As parents, we need to monitor what our children are doing. They need exercise and healthy activities that work their mind and body, not to spend all their time in front of a TV or computer screen. We also must talk about sex and the blessing of sexual purity because the most insidious attacks of the devil in our times have to do with sexual perversion. This is an important topic we will address further later in this chapter when we discuss the unique challenges of parenting teenagers.

Moral development

Morality is basically what we believe to be right and wrong. There was a time when that was simple enough; right was right and wrong was wrong. But we are living in an unprecedented time in history. Moral relativism is all around us. People are basically saying, "I'll believe what I want to believe, you believe what you want to believe, and we'll both be right." They reject absolute truth, which is a rejection of the God I serve, because He is the way, the truth, and the life (John 14:6).

Schools have been bombarding children with this ungodly moral relativism for decades. A Barna Group survey on what Americans believe asked if there was absolute truth. Sixty-six percent of adults responded that "there is no such thing as absolute truth; different people can define truth in conflicting ways and still be correct."[1] The Barna Group also found that only 20 percent of students who were highly churched as teens remained spiritually active by age twenty-nine.[2] One reason this is happening is that parents aren't establishing and modeling a belief in absolute truth at home. So when their children leave home, they are easily led astray by these humanistic beliefs.

Developing your children morally means teaching them right and wrong, and that includes setting clear boundaries (what you will and won't allow in your home) and disciplining them when they do what is wrong. Some people are wary of disciplining their children in a way that causes them injury, but physical discipline is an important part of moral development.

The Book of Proverbs gives instruction on spanking our children. It doesn't advocate beating our children and being physically abusive. That is a crime, and parents who abuse their children should be punished under the law. But proper spanking is in the Bible.

> He who spares his rod hates his son, but he who loves him disciplines him promptly.
>
> —Proverbs 13:24

Again, abuse is not what the Bible is talking about here. That is a sin. If your child does something that makes you angry, you should cool down before you administer punishment. Proverbs 22:8 says, "And the rod of his anger will fail," which means disciplining a child in anger will not have the desired effect. If you don't cool down, your children will think you are spanking them because they made you mad. You must spank your children because they disobeyed, not because they upset you, and it is critical that your children understand that distinction.

Because physical discipline can be tricky for many parents, I want to share some simple rules to follow concerning biblical spanking:

1. Determine if the offense warrants a spanking.

Scripture says, "A youngster's heart is filled with foolishness, but physical discipline will drive it far away" (Prov. 22:15, NLT). Yet spanking is not a cure-all. In fact, it should be treated as the last resort. We use verbal correction and lack of privilege before spanking. But when these methods are ineffective, biblical spanking should be our last option. It is critical that it be done carefully and deliberately for it to produce proper results. That is why following all the steps we list is critical.

2. *Give your children clear rules.*

If your children don't know the rules, how can they be expected to obey them? The Bible says, "For where there is no law there is no transgression" (Rom. 4:15). Give your children clear instruction and tell them in advance what the consequences will be if they disobey. Let's say, for example, you don't want your children to jump on the bed. First, clearly communicate that they are not to jump on the bed, and explain why. You can tell them jumping on the bed is dangerous and because you love them you don't want them to get hurt. Then let them know if they jump on the bed, they will have disobeyed you and Jesus, and their actions will force you to spank them, though you really don't like to do that.

3. *Keep your word.*

One of the important points in training a child in anything is keeping your word. Don't tell them ten or fifteen times, "If you do that one more time I am going to spank you." If you tell your child you are going to spank them, do it. If you don't follow through on what you say, your words will begin to mean nothing. You are actually, subliminally, teaching them to lie, because that's what you are doing.

4. *Before the spanking is administered, calmly explain to the child why you are doing this and make him acknowledge that he understands.*

Proverbs 29:15 says, "The rod and reproof give wisdom: but a child left to himself bringeth his mother to shame" (KJV). Ask your child, "Do you understand why I am spanking you?" He needs to tell you why in his own words. If he can't do so, you need to explain the reason for the spanking again until he understands.

When you are certain your child knows why he is being punished, it's important that you remember these guidelines:

Don't use your hand. Your hand is designed to love and care for your child.

Choose a paddle that isn't too big (a three-year-old, for instance, shouldn't be spanked with a big board but rather something about the size of a wooden spoon). The term "rod" as used in Proverbs refers to a stick or branch. When my kids were between five and twelve years old, we used a medium-sized tree branch. They have some flexibility and sting but will not physically injure them *unless* you spank them too hard.

Don't hit so hard that you cause long-term pain. You want your children to feel some discomfort but not lasting pain.

Spank your children *only* on their bottom, which is properly padded. *Never* strike your children on the face, pinch them, or punch them. This kind of "discipline" begins to cross the line to abuse.

Do not let your children jump around and scream during the spanking. Make them be still, or they could really hurt themselves.

When you are done, let them cry, but don't let them throw an angry fit. If they do, you didn't do your job properly. Psalm 51:17 says, "The sacrifices of God are a broken spirit: a broken and a contrite heart, O God, thou wilt not despise" (KJV). The purpose of correction is so your children will recognize what they did wrong and have a contrite heart. If your child throws a tantrum after being disciplined, they aren't contrite and the discipline hasn't been effective.

After they stop crying, love on them, hug them, and bring them back into fellowship. Fellowship was broken because of disobedience, so it is critical to restore lost fellowship.

Then pray with them so fellowship can be restored with the Lord. You are teaching them an important principle that some people never learn: how to repent. But make sure they are repentant and not still angry. If you have done this properly, they should not still be mad at you.

End by saying, "You understand I didn't do this because I am mad at you, but because I love you." You want to make sure they understand why they were disciplined and that you did not strike them in anger.

Once the discipline has been administered, don't bring the matter up again. When Jesus forgives He forgets.

For discipline to be effective, we must have faith that spanking is a God-ordained part of the training process. Proverbs 13:24 says, "He who spares his rod of discipline hates his son, but he who loves him disciplines diligently and punishes him early" (KJV). The heart of spanking is to teach your children to obey. The Bible tells us to honor our parents that it may be well with us and that we will live long on the earth (Eph. 6:2). This is the only command with a promise attached to it. The reason is this: You love your children dearly, but God loves them more. And when they obey you, the parent, they are learning to obey God.

If we don't lovingly but firmly discipline our children, we are doing them a disservice. They must learn that our actions carry consequences. If they don't learn that, they are open prey for the enemy to wreak havoc in their lives when they grow up. Prisons are filled with people who never learned to obey authority.

Spiritual development

Just because a child is raised in a Christian home and has parents who love Jesus, that doesn't automatically mean he will really know and walk with God on a daily basis. Your children have a free will to make their own choices. But a lot of what your children will learn about walking with God is through the example that you, Mom and Dad, set for them at home. You can tell them they need to pray, but the way they will really learn that is by watching you pray in front of them. You can tell them they need to worship Jesus, but they won't know how unless they see you do it.

I have had a habit that I have practiced for years. I love to sit in the bathtub and read the Bible. I have Bibles that are thick and all spread out because they have gotten wet so much. But it seems like the bathtub is where I meet with God. I have heard God speak to me more in the bathtub than anywhere else. Jesus said that when you pray you should go to your closet. So my prayer closet is wet, but it is where I meet with the Lord.

I've done this since my kids were little. I never really talked much about it, but my kids learned that when I was in the bathtub I was usually reading the Bible. Sometimes I would be in there over an hour. That just became my routine and still is today.

The night before my son got married, Trudi and I sat in the kitchen with him reminiscing about his life. It was a very emotional conversation as we talked about things that happened as he grew up. At one point he said, "Dad, one of the things that I'll never forget is how you read the Bible when you were in the bathtub. When you were in the bathroom for all that time it always brought me comfort to think, my dad is in there reading the Bible and talking to Jesus."

Today my son is a pastor. He has three little children and it's not always convenient, but he reads the Bible in the bathtub.

Your children's spiritual development and living relationship with Jesus can be greatly influenced by your own. The example you live before your children is everything. If you tell your children they shouldn't drink alcohol or watch certain movies but do those things yourself, your training is not going to work. If your children don't admire your life, they will not embrace your value system. Our example speaks louder than our words.

As important as your child's emotional, intellectual, physical, and moral development are, their spiritual development is most important. In the next chapter, we will zero in on specific ways you can help your children come into a relationship with Jesus and develop spiritually, even from a young age. Faith in Christ is the most important legacy you can leave your children. And helping them develop a personal faith in Christ is the most critical way you will protect them from the enemy.

A word about teenagers

Before we close this chapter, I want to share a few words about teenagers. The teenage years offer unique challenges because this is a unique time of development.

A 2004 *Time* magazine cover story titled "Secrets of the Teenage Brain" provides some interesting insight into what is going on inside teenagers during this season. Between birth and the age of five, children experience 95 percent of their brain development. Think about how much children learn in the first few years of life: language, motor skills, and so on. The brain's development continues on this track until approximately the age of ten. Then from age ten to twenty, the other 5 percent of the brain slowly develops until it reaches full maturity.[3]

But that last 5 percent of the brain is where executive decisions are made. This is the part of the brain that is able to assess risk, use logic, and make sound decisions. You don't have all this capacity until you are over the age of twenty. This is why your teenagers will do something dumb and when you ask them why they did it, they'll say, "I don't know." They really don't! The reason they don't know is that their brains aren't fully developed yet. I know you suspected that to be true, but now you have physiological evidence.[4]

I don't say this to denigrate your teenagers. I say this so that you can understand what is going on inside them. Not only are their brains not fully developed, but they are also going through major physical changes. They are being bombarded by hormones and walking through waters they have never navigated.

Many Christian parents are just too naive when it comes to understanding what their teenager is going through. I know, because I was that way. We can think that because our teenagers are Christians they won't go through the same temptations as non-Christian kids, but that is not true. There are not Christian hormones and non-Christian hormones. There are just hormones, and they come at teenagers hard. They need your help as their parents to navigate this tough time.

What makes this doubly challenging is that often they begin to pull away from you during the teen years. When they are little, mom and dad are their heroes. But as they grow up, mom and dad seem to be the most uncool people in the world. It can hurt your feelings. But understand this: when they are pushing you away on the outside, on the inside they are really saying, "Please don't let me go. I'm confused. I need help." You have to work hard at staying in their lives.

What you can't do is be too trusting. The question I am asked the most when it comes to teenagers is, "What do I do? When I try to put some restrictions in my teenager's life he says, 'Don't you trust me?'"

That is the classic teenage question, "Don't you trust me?" But remember, we are devil-proofing our children. So the answer to the "trust me" question is a resounding, "*No!*" But you should go on to explain to your child, "It's not you that I don't trust. It's the devil. He is doing all he can during these teenage years to destroy your life. Because I don't trust the devil and what he wants to do to you, I am going to monitor everything in your life."

I know some parents may think this is mean. But I believe as parents we have the right to know *everything* that is going on in our teenagers' lives. That includes monitoring their phones and social media accounts to know what they are doing and who their friends are.

You have the right to go in their room and look under the mattress and in the closet. You should have influence in what they wear. As long as they are in your home, you have the right to lovingly and firmly parent them. That means you are involved in every aspect of their life. You don't have to be an outdated prude or overly suspicious. You just need to be wise. You do this because you love and care about your teens.

When my daughter was sixteen we bought her a car of her own. I love my daughter and wanted to bless her. But I knew something. She was a cute, blonde, young lady, and I knew she wasn't ready to have the car with no restrictions. It wasn't a matter of trust. It is called parenting. We had restrictions she had to abide by.

To go out in the car, she had to accept certain rules. We wanted to know where she was going, what she was going to do there, and who she was going to be with. We set a time for her to leave and a time for her to be back.

Let's say she was going to a movie. We wanted to know what movie she planned to see. This was before the Internet and cell phones, but we would check out the rating of the movie she wanted to see before we let her go. We didn't do this every time, but sometimes we would drive over to the theater where she was seeing the movie and drive around the parking lot until we found her car. Then we would put a sticky note on the windshield saying, "So glad you are being obedient and doing what you told us. Love, Mom and Dad."

We wanted to put in her mind that, "Mom and Dad know all and see all. They are like the Holy Spirit and can be anywhere at any time. Mom and Dad are omnipresent." It's not that we didn't trust Brooke. We were monitoring and training her. It's something a good parent does. Why? Because we don't trust the devil and his strategies against our kids.

If she didn't abide by the rules she lost her privileges to the car. That was the rule. We weren't mean when we explained this, but we were firm.

One final word on this: The most insidious attacks of the devil in our times have to do with sexual perversion. As parents we must monitor our young people and their sexual development. They need their parents to help them understand what is going on physically and emotionally.

Parents need to have an initial conversation about the birds and the bees, but that is not the only time you should talk about sex. You should have an ongoing monitoring process as they grow up. As a parent you need to deliberately broach this subject, multiple times, once every few weeks. The enemy uses sexual temptation and sexual sin to destroy people's lives, and teenagers need our help as they navigate these dangerous waters.

There are many great resources to help parents address this subject with their children, including *Guardians of Purity* by Julie Hiramine and *The Focus on the Family Guide to Talking With Your Kids About Sex*. We encourage you to take advantage of these and other resources to answer the specific questions your teenagers may have.[5]

Be strong! Your children may kick and scream when you implement parental disciplines into their lives. You can't be a wimp and get the job done. Ephesians 6:10 says, "Be strong in the Lord and in his mighty power" (NLT).

Remember the devil hates your kids and is serious about destroying their lives. He wants to get a foothold when they are young and the most impressionable. But your kids don't understand this. So you have to be strong if you are going to raise kids who don't fall in step with the devil's plans for their generation.

I'm not talking about being mean. Everything we do must be motivated by love. But God is love, and He is no pushover.

If we are going to train our children to be champions for Christ we must be strong and resolute to stand against the compromise and weakness that is so pervasive in our society. This is not the time to worry about being your child's buddy. That will come later, after they have grown up. Right now, the goal is to protect them from the enemy. That includes training them as we have discussed as well as praying for them daily. Seek God about His calling on their lives, and declare His purposes over them. Below is a prayer for sons and a prayer for daughters that you can speak over your children daily. Alter it as the Holy Spirit leads with the unique promises He has given you for your child.

A PRAYER FOR SONS AND YOUNG MEN

Father, in Jesus's name, I thank You for ________________. By confessing Your Word, I release Jesus—the Word made manifest—to work on his behalf. I thank You that ________________ is a good young man, and his steps are ordered of You. Though he may fall, he won't be utterly cast down, for You will support and uphold him (Ps. 37:23–24). You teach him to profit and lead him in the way he should go (Isa. 48:17). You are his confidence, firm and strong. You keep his foot from being caught in a trap or in hidden danger (Prov. 3:26).

________________ is wise and suspects danger and cautiously avoids evil (Prov. 14:16). He chooses wise companions, and he shall be wise (Prov. 13:20). He prizes and exalts wisdom, which promotes him and brings him to honor (Prov. 4:8). He hears wisdom *and he will speak excellent and princely things. The opening of his lips shall be for right things. His mouth shall utter truth, and wrongdoing is loathsome to his lips. All his words are right. Nothing contrary to truth is in them (Prov. 8:6–8). He is a young man of understanding, drawing counsel out of his heart (Prov. 20:5). He blesses the Lord, who gives him counsel, and his heart instructs him in the night seasons (Ps. 16:7). The lines of his portion are fallen in pleasant places for him. He has a good heritage, or inheritance (Ps. 16:6).*

His gift makes room for him and brings him before great men (Prov. 18:16). Every place the sole of his foot shall tread upon shall be given to him, and no man shall stand before him all the days of his life (Josh. 1:3, 5). You, Lord, will suffer no man to do him wrong. You will reprove kings for his sake (Ps. 105:14). He has that which is desired in a man—loyalty and kindness—and his glory and delight are his giving (Prov. 19:22). You are with him; therefore, he is a prosperous young man, and all those around him are blessed for his sake (Gen. 39:2, 5). You will make him a great family and bless him with abundant increase of favors. You will make his name famous and distinguished, and he will be a blessing, dispensing good to others (Gen. 12:2). In the name of Jesus. Amen.

A Prayer for Daughters and Young Ladies

Father, in Jesus's name, I come, presenting _______________ to You. I confess that because she has made Jesus the Lord of her life and is being trained in the way she should go, even when she is old, she shall not depart from it (Prov. 22:6).

She shall be as Ruth. She will refuse to leave the God of her godly parents and to leave the principles they taught her (Ruth 1:16).

She shall be as Abigail—a strong intercessor—a woman of great understanding and of a beautiful countenance (1 Sam. 25:3).

She shall be as Esther. She shall obtain favor in the sight of all who look upon her (Esther 2:15).

Her adornment shall not be merely external, of braiding the hair, wearing of gold, or of putting on apparel, but her adornment shall be the ornament of a meek and quiet spirit, which is very precious in the sight of God (1 Pet. 3:3–4).

She is a virtuous woman. Her price is far above rubies. When she is married, her husband's heart will safely trust in her. She will do him good and not evil all the days of her life. Strength and dignity are her clothing, and she smiles at the future. She opens her mouth with wisdom. In her tongue is the law of kindness (Prov. 31:25–26).

She is as Sarah. She receives strength to conceive by the incorruptible seed—the Word of God—by faith, and she fulfills the will of God in her life, because she judges Him faithful who has promised (Heb. 11:11). She is as Mary—a handmaid of the Lord. It shall be true unto her according to God's Word, and there shall be a performance of those things told her by Him (Luke 1:38, 45). We pray these blessings over ______________ in Jesus's name, amen.

When we've done all we know to do to devil-proof our children, we must trust God to do the rest. The Bible promises that He will. Remember, the effectual, fervent prayers of the righteous availeth much (James 5:16).

Of all the keys to devil-proofing your children, the one we are about to discuss next is the most important. So get ready.

Chapter 11

INTRODUCING YOUR CHILDREN TO CHRIST

MOST PEOPLE TOTALLY underestimate the spiritual potential of children. But remember what Jesus said about them in Mark 10:

> When Jesus saw what was happening [the disciples rebuking the children for coming to Jesus], he was angry with his disciples. He said to them, "Let the children come to me. Don't stop them! For the Kingdom of God belongs to those who are like these children."
>
> —MARK 10:14, NLT

Jesus makes it clear that children can receive the kingdom of God. But what exactly does that mean? Let's look at another statement Jesus made concerning the kingdom to a Jewish religious leader named Nicodemus:

> Jesus replied, "I tell you the truth, unless you are born again, you cannot see the Kingdom of God."
>
> —JOHN 3:3, NLT

So let's put this together: Children can receive the kingdom, and you see the kingdom by being born again. The only conclusion we can draw is that children can be born again!

Children need to receive Jesus into their hearts and be born again. That is the foundation for knowing Christ. Even when they are young, they can meet Jesus and begin a relationship with Him. In fact, that is the best time to begin teaching the truths of God's Word because childhood is when a person's foundational beliefs are established. What age is ideal? We get insight from the Book of Isaiah:

> Whom shall he teach knowledge? and whom shall he make to understand doctrine? them that are weaned from the milk, and drawn from the breasts. For precept must be upon precept, precept upon precept; line upon line, line upon line; here a little, and there a little.
>
> —Isaiah 28:9–10, kjv

The most basic doctrine is being born again, and this passage lets us know "them that are weaned from the milk" are the ones we should teach basic doctrine. That's around the toddler or preschooler age. When our children are around two or three, we can begin to teach them in clear and simple terms about Jesus—who He is and what He has done for us.

Isaiah 28:10 even tells us how to do it: precept upon precept, line upon line. In other words, the younger they are the more basic we have to make it. But even if we break the gospel down into simple, childlike terms, we need to realize this is not just a cute thing we are doing. We are opening the door for our children to meet the real Jesus, even when they are little.

In the Muslim faith mothers whisper in their baby's ear, "Allah is God. Mohammed is his prophet." When their children are infants they are beginning a process of training. Allah is not the way, the truth, and the life. But they convince their children that he is. Many are so convinced of this that they commit the worst atrocities, even becoming suicide bombers, because they believe they will be rewarded for it. Such is the power of training children.

Thank God for churches that believe children can be born again, pray, worship God, and serve Him wholeheartedly. You need to go to that kind of church. But you don't have to wait for the church to begin ministering this truth to your children. As a parent, you can lead your own child to Christ. We talked about Jesus with our children from the time they were born, and we led each of them to Christ when they were three years old. Did they understand what they were doing? Yes!

Children can be filled with the Holy Spirit, and learn to hear the voice of the Holy Spirit and all the basic doctrines of Christianity. But you may be wondering, how do you talk with a child that young about the things of God? In the remainder of this chapter, I will share several principles Trudi and I have learned and practiced in our years of children's ministry.

MAKE IT FUN

Children have one goal in life: to have fun. In fact, they are deeply committed to fun and will pay a great price to have it.

When my son was around the age of eight he discovered baseball, and he loved it. He wanted to play all the time. He played in Little League, but he also played with all the little boys in our neighborhood. We liked knowing where he was, so all the boys would come over and play in our yard. They would destroy our grass and knock holes in the fence, but that's the price you pay as a parent.

Now, summers in Tulsa are very hot and humid. When Josh was having these tournaments he would get up early and begin playing. He played all morning, and we would have to make him come in and eat lunch. As soon as he ate he would go back outside and play all afternoon. We would occasionally go out and make him drink some water because we were concerned he would get dehydrated. When the sun went down, we had to make him come in the house. I can remember him sitting in the bathtub and nearly dozing off before we put him to bed because he was so exhausted. Then he would wake up in the morning and do it all over again.

Why would a little person put himself through such torture? Because he was having fun. Children are deeply committed to having fun. That's pretty much their only goal.

That's why when we talk to children about the things of God, in church and at home, we must make it a fun experience. We must be willing to get into their world. That communicates to them that we really care. The best example of someone doing this was Jesus. In order to minister to us He stooped down to become like us. He totally related to our world.

I have previously mentioned my time on *The Gospel Bill Show*. The key to that show's success was that kids had fun watching it. We taught Bible principles. Kids got saved and filled with the Spirit. We taught them about prayer, worship, and divine healing. We taught character issues and doctrine, but we made it fun. Our music was fun, and our characters were fun, and because of that children watched and they learned.

If you want children to listen to you talk about the things of God, you need to get into their world. And if you are going to get into their world, you must do something fun.

We were recently leading a meeting at a church. After the service we went to the pastor's house for a meal. He had a little two-year-old girl. She was shy, so I began asking her questions. I said, "Do you have any dollies?" She brightened up and shook her head yes. I said, "Would you show them to us?" She led me and Trudi to her room and began showing us her dolls, then she began to tell us about other things in her room. She ended up talking and showing us *everything* in her room, giving details about it all (after all, she is female).

That night at supper she wanted to sit by me. After we finished eating, I was talking to her father the pastor, and she came over and asked me, "Would you come play in my room?" Her dad had to keep saying, "No, sweetie, Pastor Blount is talking to Daddy right now." She was not being rude. She just liked me because I had shown an interest in the things she enjoyed. When Trudi and I were flying home the next day, I received a text from the pastor, saying his little girl wanted to know if we could come over and play again.

Some people might think that happened because I have a special anointing to minister to kids. No, I've just learned that if I'm going to reach them I have to first show interest in them and be willing to get on their level. When we do that we are not just saying we love them, we are proving it. This will work for children's church teachers, parents, and grandparents alike. Be real with kids and get into their world by having fun with them.

TELL YOUR STORY

Children love stories. One of the most effective ways to minister to kids is to tell them stories. Yes, they need to learn stories from the Bible, but they also need to hear stories about your life. Tell them how it was when you were growing up. Tell them about when you met Jesus. Tell them what Jesus has done for you.

When Trudi was four years old she fell and hit her head on the concrete driveway one day while running to meet her dad. It triggered a birth defect that caused her eyes to cross. She had cosmetic surgery three times growing up to correct the condition, but her eyes would always cross again after a few days.

She grew up with that condition, wearing contact lenses or thick glasses. She was pretty, but you could tell there was something not quite right with her eyes. Soon after she got saved back in the seventies, she went to a home prayer meeting one night. They were praying for different needs and somebody asked her, "Trudi, do you believe Jesus can heal your eyes?"

She replied, "Yes, I do." That was a statement of faith. They prayed for her in Jesus's name, and about an hour later her eyes began to bother her. She had her glasses on and yet her vision seemed to be blurry.

She took her glasses off and looked in the mirror. Her eyes looked straight! She put the glasses back on but again she couldn't see. So she took them off again and looked closely. Her eyes were no longer crossed! They had straightened out in an hour! She threw her glasses away. It was a miracle. Her eyes have been perfectly straight since 1971!

We have told that story thousands of times in churches and at meetings everywhere. But we have also shared it with our own children and grandchildren. I told my grandson Augustus the story when he was four. I made it exciting and told it in a simple way that he could understand. As I told him, he would make comments like, "Really, Papa? (He actually said "weawwy," because he can't pronounce his Rs.) That is awesome!"

I know very little about the history of my side of the family. My dad didn't talk much about his family when I was growing up. But it's important to talk to your children about the family history. It gives them a reference point to know where they came from, even if where they came from wasn't so good. It's just as important, if not more important, to tell your children about your spiritual history, because it gives them a sense of identity.

In Joshua 4, after God parted the Jordan River so the children of Israel could cross over on dry ground, God commanded twelve men to collect stones from the middle of the river and set them up in their camp. Why?

> When your children ask, "What do these stones mean to you?" you will answer them that the waters of the Jordan were cut off before the ark of the covenant of the Lord. When it crossed the Jordan, the waters of

> the Jordan were cut off. These stones will be a memorial for the children of Israel continually.
>
> —JOSHUA 4:6–7, MEV

These stones were to remind the next generation of what God had done, so they would know what a mighty God they served. Just like the children of Israel, your children need to hear your stories.

Before I went into ministry Trudi and I went through a really tight time financially. It was 1977. Our daughter, Brooke, was two, and I had decided to go to school and learn to cut hair so I could open up my own salon. This was back in the days when men wore their hair really long (think John Travolta in *Saturday Night Fever*). I got a grant to pay for school, but for the twelve months of my training I could only work part time to support my family.

Trudi worked a part-time job too, but our combined income was only a little over one hundred dollars a week. That was tough even in 1977. During this time we trusted God. We had no other choice. We would pay our ten dollar tithe every week to honor Jesus, and it was amazing how God took care of us.

During that same time, we bought a house from a man. He gave us favor and allowed me to defer my house payment for a year. Our next door neighbor was a little lady in her eighties. We called her Memaw George. I would be at school and Memaw George would call Trudi up and say, "Honey, I made too much supper for myself tonight. I put some mashed potatoes on your porch." She began doing that just about every day. The thing was, Memaw George was an awesome cook. I couldn't wait to get home to see what Memaw George had made us to eat.

At Christmas that year we didn't have much money. I waited until right before Christmas to buy our tree because that's when the prices dropped. The trees were pretty picked over, but

I found a tall tree that was well shaped until you got to the bottom branches. Those branches were misshapen and stuck out, but I knew I could saw them off. When I picked up the tree, it turns out all the branches had fallen off the back side. But that was OK because it would fit flat on the wall of our little living room.

We didn't have any money for ornaments, but back in those days women's Leggs panty hose came in plastic containers that were shaped like eggs. Trudi had saved a bunch of those. She hand decorated them by gluing little fabric and lace on them, and they became our Christmas ornaments. We used paper clips and hung them on the tree. God took care of us until I got out of school and opened my own shop.

We saved some of those ornaments. Now we have a very nice tree with beautiful decorations. But every year we put one of the Leggs ornaments on the tree. As our family sits around the tree to open gifts, I take the ornament and tell the story. I remind our children and grandchildren of God's faithfulness. The Bible is a book of passed-down stories. Your children and grandchildren need to hear your stories.

Answer Your Children's Questions

In my early days of ministry, I worked as a visitation pastor at a church in Fort Worth, Texas. I visited people who were new to the church, those who were sick and shut-in, and members who were in the hospital.

I had prayed for a man who was in the hospital with a heart condition, and God had healed him. His name was Mr. Dupuis. He was a French Cajun man in his seventies. He had short, curly white hair he combed straight back, and a big personality, and he and I became great friends.

A few years after I'd moved on to another church, I came back to the Fort Worth congregation to preach, and Mr. Dupuis was still there.

After the service he said, "I'd like to take your family to a really nice restaurant that serves lobster. Would that be OK?"

I said, "Yes, sir. We'll work that into our schedule."

My children were eight and four at the time and had never eaten lobster before. So they were pretty excited. At the restaurant, there was a big lobster tank in the waiting area, and my four-year-old son Joshua was fascinated with it. He began asking me question after question: "Hey, Dad, is that a real lobster?" "Hey, Dad, is that what we are going to eat?" "Hey, Dad, why does he have rubber bands on his claws?" "Hey, Dad, if I stuck my finger in that claw, would it cut my finger off?" "Hey, Dad, does it hurt when a lobster dies?"

Josh asked these questions nonstop and didn't even give me time to answer! I was trying to talk to Mr. Dupuis, and Josh kept interrupting with the questions. Even after the waitress seated us, the questions kept coming.

Finally, I said, "Joshua, be quiet. I'm trying to talk here."

I noticed Mr. Dupuis was smiling as he watched this conversation. After a while he asked me, "Does that boy ask a lot of questions?"

I said, "Are you kidding? He does this all the time."

He said, "Do you know why he asks questions?"

I didn't know what he meant. Mr. Dupuis said, "That boy is asking questions because he is only four. He doesn't know much, and he is hungry to learn. And the way he learns is by asking questions. He is asking you because you are his father. There is nobody he wants to learn from more than his dad."

I said, "Oh."

He went on, "So, as he grows up, always take the time to answer this boy's questions. Because if you don't," he paused and looked me in the eye, "he might grow up and be...stupid."

I never forgot that as my kids grew up. I think many people struggle in life because their parents didn't take the time to really listen to them and answer their questions.

You can target where your kids are mentally and spiritually by listening to the questions they ask. Did you ever notice how many times Jesus allowed people to ask Him questions? When it comes to spiritual things, answering their questions is a great way to teach them.

Allow your children to ask their questions. It is a big part of the learning process. Also, be proactive in initiating conversations with them about God and spiritual things.

If you'll go into your children's room and show interest in their world, you might be amazed at how they will open their heart and begin to talk to you—all because you got on their turf. When you show you care about them, they will open up and talk. Let them ask questions and answer them if you can. Sometimes my children would ask me about things I would have to dig into the Bible to answer. But that's a good thing!

Teach Your Children to Praise and Worship Jesus

Music is a powerful force. When it comes to the spiritual development of children, music is a God-ordained tool. There are two basic ways to use music to connect our children to God:

To teach

Colossians 3:16 says, "Let the word of Christ dwell in you richly in all wisdom, teaching and admonishing one another in psalms and hymns and spiritual songs, singing with grace in your hearts to the Lord." Notice the verse says music can be used to teach and admonish (this means to be reminded of something with a sense of obligation). Psalms is a book of songs originally sung in the temple and the synagogues.

Jewish parents used songs to teach their children to memorize Scripture. That still works. One of the best ways to remember something is to sing it.

Have you noticed that when you hear a song from your past, often you can remember every word even if you haven't heard it in a long time? That's the power of music. I've noticed that when I am going through times of challenge, if I will listen for it, I'll hear a song in my heart. The Bible says God gives "songs in the night" (Job 35:10, NLT). Music has the power to help you remember like nothing else. There are many great children's songs that teach both Bible verses and Bible stories.[1]

To welcome the presence of God

The Bible says, "Don't be drunk with wine, because that will ruin your life. Instead, be filled with the Holy Spirit, singing psalms and hymns and spiritual songs among yourselves, and making music to the Lord in your hearts" (Eph. 5:18–19, NLT). Notice the analogy. People drink wine or intoxicating drinks because they affect the way they feel. For the time they are drinking, their troubles disappear. But that feeling does not last. After they sober up nothing has changed. That's why the Bible tells us not to get drunk with alcohol.

But when you sing and praise God, you welcome the Holy Spirit into your situation. Praising God can affect and change negative circumstances! It happened over and over in the Bible. In 2 Chronicles 20, the praises of Israel brought confusion and defeat to the enemy. And in Acts 16, Paul and Silas's praises brought about a miraculous deliverance from prison. Singing and praising God in the time of trouble will release the supernatural.

Learning to worship Jesus will bring real answers and lasting results, unlike wine. This is a powerful truth. When trouble comes your way and you don't know what to do, one of the best things to do is worship. As parents we need to train our children to worship Jesus and tap into the presence of God. This is not just for church but something we can do at home.

Let me illustrate. Trudi and I moved to Tulsa, Oklahoma, from Texas in 1982. We enrolled our daughter, who was six, in a Christian school. She had been in a small kindergarten class of six children in Texas, and the school she would be attending in Tulsa had over two thousand students.

Brooke was a sweet, quiet little girl, and her new school was as big as the previous town we had lived in. Looking back it was just too much of a change for her little psyche.

I took her to school that first day. Not long after I arrived at work, I received a call from the principal, "Mr. Blount, we need you to come pick Brooke up. She's sick and throwing up."

I picked her up to take her home, but as soon as we left the parking lot she was playing in the backseat of the car and everything seemed to be fine. She went home and ate lunch and played normally the rest of the afternoon.

We thought she must have had a short-lived bug. So the next morning I took her back to class, and about the same time as the day before, I got another call from the principal. "Mr. Blount, your daughter is throwing up again."

Repeat the scene from day one. As soon as I come she's playing in the backseat, eating lunch; everything is fine. My lightning-fast mind began to figure this out. She wasn't sick. Something about school was making her so afraid she was getting sick. It was fear. I realized we had to help her deal with it, because she had to go to school.

I got an idea. I looked in Brooke's toy box and got one of her little girl dolls. I needed a villain figure too. The most sinister character I could find was a smiling lion, but that would have to do.

After we ate dinner that night, I gathered the whole family

around the fireplace and got behind the couch to do a skit for the kids. First, I had the little girl doll come up.

Doll: "This is the first day in my brand-new school. I'm a little nervous. I wonder what this will be like."

Then I had the lion, who represented the devil, come up. He began to talk to the little girl in a sinister voice.

Lion: "Hey, kid. There are a lot of kids here in this new school."

Girl: "There sure are a lot of kids in this school."

Lion: "Yeah, kid. They are probably going to think you are weird."

Girl: "What if they think I'm weird?"

Lion: "Yeah, kid. They aren't going to like you."

Girl: "What if they don't like me?"

Lion: "You are getting so scared your stomach is getting upset."

Girl: "I am so afraid. I think my stomach is getting upset."

Lion: "Yeah, kid. You are going to throw up."

Girl: "I think I'm going to throw up!" (Doll begins to gag.)

The lion begins to laugh. "Ha ha! I've made this little girl so nervous she is going to throw up. I love to make kids afraid and sick."

Then the little girl comes to her senses.

Girl: "Wait a minute. These are thoughts of fear coming against me."

Lion: "No, this is the truth. Nobody will like you!"

Girl: "I know what this is. This is the devil trying to make me afraid."

Lion: "You're wrong, kid. You really are weird."

Girl: "No, this is the devil. The Bible says when I praise God I will stop the devil from bothering me. So I am going to praise the Lord right now!"

Lion: "Oh, no. Don't do that, kid!"

Girl: "Hallelujah. I praise You, Lord. God hasn't given me the spirit of fear, but of power, love, and a sound mind. Glory to God!"

Lion: "No! Please don't do that."

Girl: "Praise the Lord. I love You, Jesus."

Lion: "I can't stay here! I have to leave. In fact, I'm getting sick to my stomach."

(Lion begins to gag and drops behind couch.)

Girl: "I don't feel afraid anymore! The fear went away! It works! When I praise God it runs the devil away from my life. Praise the Lord!"

After I finished the skit, Brooke asked me, "Daddy, was that skit about me?"

I said, "Well, maybe. I'll tell you what we are going to do. As a family right now we are all going to praise the Lord. If there is any fear trying to come against us, we are going to run it off."

I played some recorded worship music, and we all began to sing and praise the Lord as a family. Trudi and I set the example as we walked around the room singing, lifting our hands, and even dancing as we praised the Lord. Brooke joined in, doing whatever we did. Even little, two-year-old Joshua sang and praised with us.

After we sang just a couple of songs, we could see something happening to Brooke. She became so enthusiastic. We could literally see the anointing and presence of God come on her.

Later that night when I was tucking Brooke into bed, she just kept talking about the skit and saying, "Praise the Lord, Daddy. Isn't God good?"

As I pulled the covers up she looked at me with her sweet little green eyes and said, "Daddy, I'm never going to be afraid again."

The next day I took her to school. When I got to my office at work, I watched the phone. But it never rang. The principal never called. Trudi picked her up that afternoon. When I came home from work that evening, I asked Brooke, "How was school today, honey?"

She said, "It was great, Daddy. I met new friends," and then she began to tell me about her classes, what she had for lunch, and all the other details of her day.

I never had to pick her up from school because she was afraid again. She learned that praising God is the trigger to release the presence of God.

Fast-forward twenty years. Brooke was married and had just learned that she was expecting her first baby. She was about six weeks into the pregnancy, and she and her husband, Scott, were in the Colorado mountains on vacation when we got a call from Scott saying Brooke was having some concerning symptoms and something might be wrong.

Within a few hours she had lost the baby. I called Scott in the hotel room after it happened to check on her, and I'll never forget what he told me. "She is actually in the bathroom right now," he said. "I can hear her through the door, and she is singing and praising God."

She wasn't praising God because she lost her baby. She was praising God because at six years old she learned that when you go through times of trouble, you sing to the Lord. And your song will release the presence of God to help you. One year later, she delivered her first baby girl. God has blessed their family with two beautiful daughters who are now teenagers.

When I encourage you to teach your children to run to God and praise Him to release His presence, I am not telling you something I just made up. Jesus taught this principle. Matthew 21 gives us the account of the last few days before the Crucifixion. When Jesus entered Jerusalem on the back of a donkey, the entire city turned out to greet Him. People lined the streets and followed Him, declaring, "Hosanna to the son of David." Their praise welcomed Him to town.

Jesus then entered the temple and drove out all the money changers. After He cleaned up the house of God, the miraculous power of God began to flow.

> Then the blind and the lame came to Him in the temple, and He healed them. But when the chief priests and scribes saw the wonderful things that He did, and the children crying out in the temple and saying, "Hosanna to the Son of David!" they were indignant.
>
> —Matthew 21:14–15

The chief priests and scribes were the religious hierarchy of the day. They represented dead, powerless religion. Jesus came to expose false religion and demonstrate what God was really like. Notice the two things that upset them:

1. The blind and lame were getting healed.
2. Children were saying, "Hosanna to the son of David."

The children were praising God. Where did they learn to praise God? By watching their parents.

> They asked Jesus, "Do you hear what these children are saying?" "Yes," Jesus replied. "Haven't you ever read the Scriptures? For they say, 'You have taught children and infants to give you praise.'"
>
> —Matthew 21:16

Children are imitators. They were just copying their parents. So we could say there are two things that make the devil very nervous: the miraculous and kids praising Jesus.

I love Jesus's answer to the religious leaders. In essence He told them, "Haven't you boys ever read the Bible?" These were the religious experts of the day. They were supposed to know the law. But Jesus humbled them by quoting a scripture that was actually from Psalm 8:

> Out of the mouth of babes and nursing infants You have ordained strength, Because of Your enemies, That You may silence the enemy and the avenger.
>
> —PSALM 8:2

The word *strength* means loud, power, might, and boldness. Jesus was saying that when we train our children to praise the Lord—our little children and even our nursing infants—it releases God's power. And get this: even the praise of a little child can shut the mouth of the devil. It "silence[s] the enemy and the avenger." I didn't say this. God did.

Why does praise silence the enemy? Because it brings the power of the Holy Spirit on the scene. The devil can't stand in God's presence. He has to shut his ugly mouth when God shows up. He has to exit. I don't think the Lord likes bullies. The devil is a loudmouth bully, and when somebody will use their faith, even a child, he has to leave.

Don't you know that is humiliating to him? This is why the devil got so mad that day in John 21! He knew these children worshipping Jesus would be, as we say in Texas, a burr in his saddle for the rest of their lives.

If we want to devil-proof our children, one of the best things we can do as parents and grandparents is to set an example of praise and worship. I believe the devil has nightmares and panic attacks about families who know how to praise their way through the challenges of life.

One of the important things our ministry does is produce

praise and worship music. We produce DVDs and CDs that are designed especially for children. Kids listen to them at home, and churches use them to lead worship in kid's classes. It is one of the most important arms of our ministry. Children need to learn to praise the Lord, because it silences the enemy.

It's Never Too Soon

It's never too early to teach your children about God.

Pray continually over your children, even before they are born.

It has been proven that babies can hear from the womb. Before they are born pray Psalm 127:3 and Psalm 139:14–17 over your children:

> *Father, in Jesus's name, I thank You for my baby. I believe this is a gift from God and I receive this baby as a reward from heaven. I thank You that my baby is fearfully and wonderfully made. My baby is being perfectly constructed to be sound and healthy in the darkness of the womb. You see my baby before he/she is born. All the days of his/her life are being recorded in Your book. How precious are Your thoughts toward my baby. They are so vast they cannot be numbered.*

From the time they are born, talk to them about Jesus.

Whisper to them, "Jesus loves you and died on the cross for you. You are going to know Jesus from a young age. No weapon formed against you will prosper (Isa. 54:17). No evil will conquer you, and no plague will come against our home. The angels of the Lord will protect you wherever you go" (Ps. 91:10–11).

When they are big enough to sit up, show them a little Bible.

Tell them, "This is the Bible. These are the words of Jesus. Jesus loves you. We love Jesus's Word." Then take the Bible and hug it and kiss it for them as an example. Give them the Bible and let them hug and kiss it. You are training them in the importance of God's Word.

Pray that their hearts will be open to Christ.

Pray this prayer from Ephesians 1:17–18 and Acts 16:31 over your children to prepare their heart to receive Jesus at the right time:

> *Father, in Jesus's name, I pray for (children's names). I pray that You would give them the spirit of wisdom and revelation in the knowledge of Jesus Christ. I ask that the eyes of their understanding may be flooded with light, that they would know what is the hope of Your calling in their lives. I declare that because I believe in the Lord I will be saved, and also my house, including (children's names), in Jesus's name, amen.*

Patiently talk to your toddler and preschooler about Jesus on a regular basis.

Christian bookstores have Bibles and books that will help you talk to your children about Jesus when they are small. Ask God to lead you to a time when they are open to receive Christ. We prayed with both of our children to receive Christ when they were near the end of the age of three.

When they understand what it means to accept Christ and want to be saved, pray with them.

Have them repeat after you as you pray:

> *I believe Jesus is the Son of God. I believe Jesus died on the cross for my sin. But Jesus didn't stay dead. Jesus rose from the dead and defeated death for me. I believe in my heart and say with my mouth that Jesus is my*

Lord. From this day forward, I am born again. I am a new creature in Jesus Christ. I am God's child and on my way to heaven. Amen!

Celebrate your children's decision for Christ.

Have a birthday cake with candles that they can blow out (children love to blow out candles), and tell them that now they have two birthdays: their spiritual birthday and their natural birthday. Every year celebrate both birthdays. You may even want to make a certificate bearing the name of your child and the date he was born again. You can frame it and hang it on the wall of their room.

From time to time talk about the certificate. As you frequently talk about Jesus and the time your children received Him, it establishes in their mind the significance of their decision. The more you discuss it the more real it will be to them.

Pray with your children and read them Bible stories.

Tell them stories about what Jesus has done for you personally and talk to them about Jesus often. You will be amazed at the spiritual things they will be able to understand as you spend the time to train them.

As Spirit-filled believers, Trudi and I always believed our children could be baptized in the Holy Spirit, even at a young age. This experience is separate from salvation. Jesus said:

> And I will ask the Father, and he will give you another Advocate, who will never leave you. He is the Holy Spirit, who leads into all truth. The world cannot receive him, because it isn't looking for him and doesn't recognize him. But you know him, because he lives with you now and later will be in you.
>
> —John 14:16–17, NLT

The world can receive Christ, but not the Holy Spirit. The one who receives the baptism in the Holy Spirit is someone who is saved first. Jesus's disciples were born again when Jesus appeared to them after the Resurrection (John 20:21–22). But before Jesus left the earth, He told them to wait to be baptized in the Spirit (Acts 1:5, 8). And when the disciples were baptized with the Spirit, they spoke in a new language, and they were filled with boldness to be a witness and live for Christ. (See Acts 2:1–4.)

Just as salvation is for children so is the baptism in the Holy Spirit. Peter talked about it when he preached in Jerusalem on the Day of Pentecost:

> And it shall come to pass in the last days, saith God, I will pour out of my Spirit upon all flesh: and *your sons and your daughters* shall prophesy, and your young men shall see visions, and your old men shall dream dreams...For the promise is unto you, *and to your children,* and to all that are afar off, even as many as the Lord our God shall call.
>
> —ACTS 2:17, 39, KJV, EMPHASIS ADDED

He mentioned that the outpouring of the Holy Spirit was for your "sons and daughters," and he said the promise was "to your children." If we will instruct them and work with them at home, children can be filled with the Holy Spirit. In fact, the home is the perfect environment to pray with your children and disciple them in this important doctrine of the church.

Through the years I have led thousands of children to receive the baptism in the Holy Spirit. When your child is around the age of four, if he has accepted Christ, carefully explain what it means to be filled with the Holy Spirit.

First tell them the purpose for being filled with the Spirit—that Jesus wants them to be filled with the Spirit so that they can be bold to stand up against temptation and tell other people about Him. Then pray with your children, first emphasizing these two points:

1. They must ask (Luke 11:11, 13).

Before you pray, emphasize that they must believe God wants them to be filled with His Spirit, and they must ask Him to fill them. I often use this example. My son likes to lift weights. When he comes home he is really hungry. If I had some fresh baked bread and was putting butter on it when my son came in, hungry from lifting weights, and he asked me for some, I wouldn't say, "No, eat this rock I just got out of the yard!" No, a good father wouldn't do that. In the same way, when we ask the heavenly Father for the Holy Spirit, He will give us the Holy Spirit.

This helps alleviate the doubt that God will not give them the Holy Spirit.

2. They must speak.

Acts 2:4 says, "And they were all filled with the Holy Ghost, and began to speak with other tongues, as the Spirit gave them utterance" (KJV). I will often read that verse with children and then ask them, "Who did the talking that day? Was it the Holy Spirit, or was it the disciples?" Most of the time they will say it was the Holy Spirit.

But if you read that verse again, it says they were all filled and began to speak. It doesn't say the Holy Spirit began to speak. It says "they," the disciples, began to speak.

I do this to stress that the Holy Spirit won't make them speak. They have to use their own voice and initiate the words. When they begin to make noise, then the Holy Spirit gives them the words at the exact time. It is their voice and God's words coming out their mouth.

I also emphasize that they won't understand what they are

saying. It is like they are speaking in a secret language—God's secret language for them.

When they understand those two important points, you can lead them in this prayer:

> *Father, I thank You that I am Your child. You promised that You would fill me with the Holy Spirit if I would ask. I ask You now to baptize me in the Holy Spirit. I receive a brand-new language that is from You. Thank You for this secret language that I can use to talk to You. In Jesus's name, amen.*

At this point, instruct them not to pray in English anymore. Tell them to use their voice and begin praying in the new language with the funny sounding words the Holy Spirit gives them. Encourage them by letting them hear you pray in tongues.

After they receive the baptism in the Holy Spirit, encourage them to use their prayer language every day. You can set an example by spending a few minutes each day praying with them in the Spirit.

None of our efforts to devil-proof our children are as important as this one. Our children must develop their own relationship with the Lord, because we will not always be there to pray for them, encourage them, or tell them which path to take. It is Jesus who purchased our victory over Satan—and that includes our children's victory. Once they begin a relationship with Him, the devil will get really nervous. He may even throw a fit.

He won't leave them alone. He'll try to get them to doubt God's Word or to test the limits you set at home or even to rebel. But if you put into practice the principles we've been sharing throughout this book (particularly in chapters 9 and 10), you can protect your children from the enemy's attacks.

Teaching your children the things of God and training them to follow His ways is not easy. There is no two ways about it. But it's worth it, because there is blessing in obedience—and not just for you children. Keep reading and we'll explain what we mean.

Chapter 12

BUILD A DYNASTY

THERE IS NO doubt that devil-proofing your family is hard work. We live in the most "I want it now, what have you done for me lately" time in the history of the world. Many people don't have the patience or foresight to invest the time it takes to protect their marriage and children from the enemy's attacks. They aren't looking far enough down the road.

The Book of Exodus tells the story of the Hebrews' deliverance from slavery in Egypt. The Jewish people grew in numbers, and the Egyptians began to fear them, so they made them slaves. But the more the bondage increased, the more God blessed His people and the more they multiplied.

Because of this multiplication, Pharaoh gave these demonic orders to the Hebrew midwives Shiphrah and Puah:

> "When you help the Hebrew women as they give birth, watch as they deliver. If the baby is a boy, kill him; if it is a girl, let her live." But because the midwives feared God, they refused to obey the king's orders. They allowed the boys to live, too. So the king of Egypt called for the midwives. "Why have you done this?" he demanded. "Why have you allowed the boys to live?"
>
> —EXODUS 1:16–18, NLT

The midwives replied:

> "The Hebrew women are not like the Egyptian women... They are more vigorous and have their babies so quickly that we cannot get there in time." So God was good to the midwives, and the Israelites continued to multiply, growing more and more powerful. And because the midwives feared God, he gave them families of their own.
>
> —Exodus 1:19–21, NLT

The midwives had the strength of character to defy Pharaoh's decree. They feared God more than man. They had the mettle to do the right thing in the face of great pressure. Because of their stand, God blessed them. You could say it this way: because they chose to devil-proof these families in the face of the opposition, it opened the door for God to take care of them.

In the King James Version, verse 21 says, "God gave them houses." Remember that the word *house* can often be substituted with the word *family*. In fact, the New Living Translation says, "He gave them families of their own."

There's a rich lesson for us in the story of Shiphrah and Puah. So let's look a little more closely at these women.

According to the Chumash, the rabbinical commentary of the Torah, God rewarded the midwives for their devotion by giving them houses. These "houses" were not buildings; they were dynasties. Shiphrah (another name for Jochebed, the mother of Moses) became the ancestress of priesthood and the Levitical line, and Puah (Moses's sister Miriam) became an ancestress of the royal family that included King David.[1]

Because these women were faithful to God and not Pharaoh, God gave them dynasties. Out of Jochebed's lineage came the line of priests, and Miriam's produced David and the line of kings. So we could say that their obedience affected generations of people and produced a succession of kings and priests, which ultimately produced the Messiah, Jesus Christ.

The faithfulness of our Lord Jesus Christ continues in a line of kings and priests today. It's called the church—"And have made us kings and priests to our God; and we shall reign on the earth" (Rev. 5:10).

My point is this: your obedience to apply these principles to devil-proof your marriage and children will cause blessing to come to you. Training your children will affect them for the rest of their lives and then your grandchildren after them. After your life is done, your faithfulness to devil-proof your family will bear fruit to succeeding generations, who you will one day have with you in eternity. I close with this true story. Lucy Christina Robison was born on November 17, 1893, the daughter of Ruth and Samuel Robison, who was a circuit preacher. She was a beautiful girl with long, wavy black hair, blue eyes, and an eighteen-inch waist without a corset.

She married a cowboy named Oscar Reimer when she was eighteen on March 12, 1912. Her husband had come from Germany to America and landed at Ellis Island in 1884 when he was four years old. He could not read or write.

They migrated south to a little town in Texas called Dallas and later to the Oklahoma Territory. The times were tough in the Oklahoma territory, and Lucy and Oscar lived a hard life. They had ten children and lost five of them to sickness and other unfortunate events. But their house was filled with faith and love. One of their favorite things to do at night was sit around the fire as Lucy read the Bible to the family while Oscar churned butter.

Every week Lucy would get all the children ready, and they would pile into the wagon and make the long trip to church. One day at church, there was a young man leading worship. His name was Bo. He noticed one of the Reimers' daughters, Katherine, at the back of the church, and wanted to get to know her. They eventually got married and had five children of their own. They did the best they could to raise their children for Christ. And just when they thought they were done having children, a surprise came their way. She was a little girl they named Trudi.

Lucy never traveled far from the Oklahoma territory, but because of the influence of her circuit preacher father she was faithful to teach her children the things of God as best she knew how. Her daughter, Katherine, followed her mother's example when she became a wife and mother.

As you may have guessed, Trudi married a young man named Ken. Their marriage started out rough, but because of the heritage of faith Trudi had been given, they both met Christ. They have since traveled the world preaching the gospel and touching millions of lives with the gospel. And now their children are carrying on the legacy.

I challenge you to lift your eyes past the distractions of the moment. In the light of eternity those problems will be a blip on the screen. But what you do to invest Jesus in your family will last. Incredible fruit can be born if you will choose to act. It's worth it. I dare you. Devil-proof your family.

Appendix

PRAYERS TO DECLARE OVER YOUR FAMILY

There is power in praying God's Word over your family. The Bible tells us that God's Word is living and active; it is sharper than any two-edged sword (Heb. 4:12). On top of that, Isaiah 55:11 says it will not return void but will accomplish that for which it is sent.

In this appendix we have included several prayers for you to pray over your family. We wrote these prayers as declarations. That means that as you pray these prayers, you will be speaking God's Word and His promises over your family. You will be prophesying over your situation. In some cases, you may be thanking God in advance for what He is going to do in your spouse or children. God's Word will not return void but will accomplish that for which it is sent, so as you continually declare God's Word over your family, you can expect to see results.

While it is fine for you to pray these prayers and blessings just as they are written, we encourage you to alter them to fit your unique circumstances. Let the Holy Spirit lead you. If He drops specific promises into your spirit to pray over your family, don't ignore those nudges, even if they don't seem to make sense. Praying God's Word over your family is a powerful act, and you will see change as you remain faithful in prayer.

A Prayer for the Family

Father, in the name of Jesus, we give You thanks for our home and our family. We invite You into our home today. According to Proverbs 24:3–4, we declare that through skillful and godly wisdom our home and family are built, and by understanding they are established, by knowledge shall the chambers be filled with all pleasant and precious riches.

We confess that we're the head and not the tail; we're above and not beneath. We're blessed coming in and blessed going out (Deut. 28:6–13). No weapon formed against this home shall prosper, and every tongue that rises up in judgment against us, we show to be in the wrong (Isa. 54:17, AMP*). We shall remain fixed and stable under the shadow of the Almighty, whose power no foe can withstand (Ps. 91:1). We are hidden from the strife of tongues and the plots of man (Ps. 31:20). The Lord is our confidence, firm and strong, and shall keep our feet from being caught in a trap or hidden danger (Prov. 3:26,* AMP*).*

In every area of our home the needs of our family are met—physically, mentally, and spiritually—according to Your riches in glory by Christ Jesus (Phil. 4:19). All of our wants are met, for the Lord is our Shepherd, and we shall not want (Ps. 23:1). We live in safety and no evil or accident shall befall us, neither shall any plague come nigh our dwelling, for You have given Your angels charge over us to keep us in all our ways (Ps. 91:10–11). In our pathway is life, and there is no death (Prov. 12:28). We live in health because Jesus took our infirmities and bore our sicknesses (Matt. 8:17). We have wisdom, because Jesus was made unto us wisdom, righteousness, sanctification, and redemption (1 Cor. 1:30).

We obtain favor in the sight of everyone who looks upon us (Esther 2:15). We have peace, for the peace of God which passes all understanding keeps our hearts and minds through Christ Jesus (Phil. 4:17). We have joy, for the joy of knowing the Lord is our strength (Neh. 8:10). God is on our side, so who can be against us (Rom. 8:31)? You have given unto us all things that pertain to life and godliness (2 Pet. 1:3), and Your love has been shed abroad in our hearts by the Holy Ghost (Rom. 5:5). With what measure we meet, it shall be measured unto us (Luke 6:38). Whether we sow time, money, prayer, or encouragement, we shall reap a bountiful harvest. God's grace has been made to abound toward us, and we have all sufficiency in all things. We abound to all good works (2 Cor. 9:6, 8).

We thank You for giving our family daily bread, and we ask for bread for others (Luke 11:3, 5). As for us and our house, we shall serve the Lord (Josh. 24:15). We shall serve You with joyfulness and gladness of heart for the abundance of all things; therefore, we shall never serve the enemy or be in hunger, thirst, nakedness, or the want of all things (Deut. 28:47, 48). In Jesus's name, amen. So be it.

A BLESSING FOR HUSBANDS

Father, in the name of Jesus, I thank You for my husband. I bless him as the head of our home and leader of our family. I thank You that my husband loves me as Christ loved the church and gave Himself up for her. I submit to him and the mission you have called us to as a couple and as a family (Eph. 5:22–24) and he submits himself to You. I declare that we shall live together in perfect unity and will love, honor, serve, and respect each other for Your glory (1 Thess. 5:13). We will not return evil for evil or insult for insult, but we will bless each other.

I declare that like the sons of Issachar, my husband is a mighty man of valor and a steadfast leader in our home. I bless his leadership and thank You for giving him the mind of Christ (1 Cor. 2:16). My husband will glorify God (1 Chron. 16:28), and our family shall be blessed.

I thank You that my husband is a good man and his steps are ordered of You. Though he fall, he won't be utterly cast down, for You will support and uphold him (Ps. 37:23–24). You teach him to profit and lead him in the way he should go (Isa. 48:17). You are his confidence, firm and strong. You keep his foot from being caught in a trap or in hidden danger (Prov. 3:26).

My husband is wise and suspects danger and cautiously avoids evil (Prov. 14:16). He prizes and exalts wisdom, which promotes him and brings him to honor (Prov. 4:8). He hears wisdom and he will speak excellent things. His mouth shall utter truth, and wrongdoing is loathsome to his lips. He blesses the Lord, who gives him counsel, and his heart instructs him in the night seasons (Ps. 16:7). The lines of his portion are fallen in pleasant places for him. He has a good heritage (Ps. 16:6), and his gift makes room for him and brings him before great men (Prov. 18:16).

Every place the sole of his foot shall tread upon shall be given to him, and no man shall stand before him all the days of his life (Josh. 1:3, 5). You, Lord, are with him; therefore, he is prosperous, and our family is blessed for his sake (Gen. 39:2, 5). You will bless him with abundant increase of favor. You will make his name famous and distinguished, and he will be a blessing, dispensing good to others (Gen. 12:2). I thank You for having good plans for my husband and our family (Jer. 29:11). I declare that we shall enjoy life and see good days (1 Pet. 3:10), in Jesus's name, amen.

A BLESSING FOR WIVES

Father, in the name of Jesus, I thank You for my wife. I love and bless her as the heart of our home. I thank You that her mind is steadfast because she trusts in You. You keep her in perfect peace (Isa. 26:3). I declare that she will always live in safety and not fear evil because she listens to You (Prov. 1:33).

My wife's adornment is not merely external—the ornament of braided hair or gold or pearls or costly array—but she has the beauty of a gentle and quiet spirit, which is precious in Your sight (1 Pet. 3:4). She is a virtuous woman. Her price is far above rubies. My heart safely trusts in her. She does me good and not evil all the days of my life. Strength and dignity are her clothing, and she smiles at the future. She opens her mouth with wisdom. In her tongue is the law of kindness (Prov. 31:25–26).

I thank You, Lord, that we shall live together in perfect unity and will love, honor, serve, and respect each other for Your glory (1 Thess. 5:13). We will not return evil for evil or insult for insult, but we will bless each other.

I declare that like Abigail, my wife is a woman of wisdom who diligently seeks You in prayer (1 Sam. 25:3). And like Esther, she shall obtain favor in the sight of all who look upon her (Esther 2:15). Like Sarah, she receives strength to conceive by the incorruptible seed—the Word of God—by faith, and she fulfills the will of God in her life, because she judges Him faithful who has promised (Heb. 11:11). She is as Mary—a handmaid of the Lord. It shall be true unto her according to God's Word, and You shall bring to pass those things You have told her (Luke 1:38, 45).

Thank You, Lord, for filling my wife with the knowledge of Your will through all spiritual wisdom and understanding, that she lives a life worthy of You and pleases You in every way. I thank You that she is bearing fruit in every good work, growing in the knowledge of You, and being strengthened with all power according to Your glorious might, for her endurance and patience (Col. 1:9–11). I pray that she, being rooted and established in Your love, will always grasp how wide and long and high and deep is Your love, and that she would be filled to the measure of all of Your fullness (Eph. 3:14–21). I pray these blessings over my wife in the precious name of Jesus, amen.

A Prayer for an Unborn Child and Childbirth

Father, in the name of Jesus, we come before You claiming our rights and privileges concerning this pregnancy and childbirth. We believe that what we confess out of Your Word will not return void, but it will accomplish that which You please and will prosper in the thing to which it is sent (Isa. 55:11). On the authority of Your Word, we say that everything concerning this pregnancy will prosper and come to full maturity (Ps. 1:3, AMP). You said You would perfect that which concerns us (Ps. 138:8). You will strengthen the bars of this mother's gates and bless the child within her (Ps. 147:13). Blessed is she among women, and blessed is the fruit of her womb, for this baby belongs to You (Luke 1:42). We declare that this baby shall be in perfect health; the Lord will make this child the head and not the tail (Deut. 28:13).

This mother shall be saved in childbearing because she continues in faith and charity and holiness with sobriety (1 Tim. 2:15). She shall not labor in vain nor bring forth for trouble, for she is the seed of the blessed of the Lord, and her offspring with her (Isa. 65:23). When she is in delivery, You shall free her when she is hemmed in and enlarge her when she is in distress (Ps. 4:1). You have not given her the spirit of fear but of power, love, and of a calm, sound mind (2 Tim. 1:7). She shall be vigorous and quickly delivered (Exod. 1:19).

Blessed shall she be when she goes in, and blessed shall she be when she goes out (Deut. 28:6). Thank You, Lord, that because she believes You, there shall be a performance of those things which You have spoken over her and this child (Luke 1:45). In Jesus's name, amen.

A Prayer for the Salvation of Loved Ones

Father, in the name of Jesus, we come before You this day on behalf of our loved ones, ________________. We believe they are gifts from You. It is written in

Your Word that Jesus came to seek and to save the lost (Luke 19:10). You are long-suffering toward our loved ones and You are not willing that any should perish, but that they all should come to repentance (2 Pet. 3:9). Your will for our loved ones—and for all men—is that they would be saved and come unto the knowledge of the truth (1 Tim. 2:4).

Satan, in the name of Jesus, we take authority over you. We bind you from the lives of our loved ones, ________________, and we loose you from your assignments against them (Matt. 18:18). You will no longer be able to blind the minds of ____________________. Our loved ones now are free to see the light of the glorious gospel of Christ shining unto them (2 Cor. 4:4).

We now ask the Lord of the harvest to send the perfect laborers into the lives of our loved ones—laborers who will present the gospel in such a way that our loved ones will listen and understand and be able to escape the snare of the devil (Matt. 9:38; 2 Tim. 2:26). Father, Your Word says You will even deliver the ones for whom we intercede who are not innocent; yes, they will be delivered through the cleanness of our hands (Job 22:30). We see our loved ones saved, filled with Your Spirit, and walking in the knowledge of the truth. We thank You, Lord, for this, and we praise You. We commit ____________________ into Your hands, in Jesus's name. Amen.

A Prayer for Protection

Father, in the name of Jesus, we thank You for divine protection. We believe that we dwell safely and shall be quiet from the fear of evil, because we hearken unto wisdom (Prov. 1:33). The Lord will keep our going out and our coming in (Ps. 121:8). Blessed are we when we come in, and blessed are we when we go out (Deut. 28:6). When we lie down, we will not be afraid, and our sleep will be sweet (Prov. 3:24). We will lie down in peace and sleep: for You, Lord, make us dwell in safety (Ps. 4:8). We will not be afraid of the terror by night, or the arrow that flies by day, or of the pestilence or destruction. A thousand shall fall at our side, and ten thousand at our right hand, but it shall not come near us (Ps. 91:5–7).

The wicked will not lie in wait against the dwelling of the righteous (Prov. 24:15). You, Lord, are our shield and high tower, our refuge and Savior. You save us from violence (2 Sam. 22:3–4). As we travel, we confess that we go on our way safely. No evil or accident shall befall us, neither shall any plague or calamity come near our dwelling. For You have given Your angels charge over us, to keep us in all of our ways. The Lord is our refuge; the Most High is our dwelling place (Ps. 91:9–11).

Your Word says, "Sufficient to the day is the evil thereof." We take authority over all evil intended for us today and we bind the plans and the works of the enemy (Matt. 6:34; 18:18). We shall tread upon the lion and the adder, the young lion and the dragon—the devil—we trample under our feet (Ps. 91:13). Many evils confront the righteous, but You deliver us out of them all (Ps. 34:19). We will call upon You, Lord, and You will answer us. You will be with us in trouble, You will deliver us, and You will honor us (Ps. 91:15). You prepare a table for us in the in presence of our enemies (Ps. 23:5). You, Lord, are our Guardian, and we are protected from tragedy. You will preserve and protect us from all evil (Ps. 121:5–7). In Jesus's name, amen!

A Prayer for Future Mates

Father, in Jesus's name, I thank You that You will perfect that which concerns me (Ps. 138:8). Your Word says that before I could breathe, You knew me. You scheduled every day of my life and You wrote it in Your book (Ps. 139:16)! So I know You have a plan for my life. You care about my future.

You said if I delight myself in You, You would give me the desires of my heart (Ps. 37:4). Your Word says that it is not good for me to be alone (Gen. 2:18), and I believe it is in Your will for me to be married. I thank You now for my future mate. I know somewhere on this earth my mate already exists. I ask You for the perfect partner and complement for my life, a person who is born again, led by Your Spirit, and will follow You wholeheartedly.

You said the steps of a good man or woman are ordered of You (Ps. 37:23). I believe as I continue to love You, serve You, and follow You, You will lead and guide me by Your Spirit. When the time is right, I will have the wisdom, discernment, and discretion to know when I have found the person who is compatible for me. I now cast all my care on You—all my anxieties and worries—because You care for me (1 Pet. 5:7). I release to You all wounds from past relationships and wipe the slate clean. I am confident that You love me. You think thoughts about me—thoughts that are not evil, but only of peace to give me an expected end (Jer.

29:11). Thank You, Lord, for my future mate, in Jesus's name, amen.

A PRAYER FOR GOD'S PERFECT PLAN FOR YOUR FAMILY

Father, we come to You today, thanking You for the plan You have for our marriage and family. We were not accidents, but we were chosen in Christ before the foundation of the world and destined to be adopted as Your own children in Christ Jesus (Eph. 1:4–5). Your Word says that before we were ever born—before we were in our mother's womb—we were Your chosen instruments (Jer. 1:5). Before we could breathe, You knew us. You scheduled every day of our lives and wrote them in Your book (Ps. 139:16). You love us and think thoughts about us—thoughts and plans that are not evil, but thoughts only of peace, to give us an expected end, a future, and a hope (Jer. 29:11).

We will stay connected and attached to You by Your Word and Your Spirit. We are so precious to You that Your Word says You indelibly imprinted, or tattooed, a picture of us on the palm of each of Your hands (Isa. 49:16). We believe we are special. We are a chosen generation, a royal priesthood (1 Pet. 2:9), and a people to be envied. The Bible prophets and kings longed to see what we see and hear (Luke 10:23–24). We were created for Your pleasure and purpose (Rev. 4:11). We will fight the good fight. We will finish our course. We will keep the faith (2 Tim. 4:7). We will press toward the mark (concealed goal) for the prize of the high calling in Christ Jesus (Phil. 3:14) by abiding in Your Word and keeping Your commandments to show You our love (John 14:21).

We will build ourselves up, founded on our most holy faith. We will make progress and rise like an edifice, higher and higher, praying in the Holy Spirit (Jude 20). We will receive the end of our faith with joy unspeakable and full of glory (1 Pet. 1:8–9). We are more than conquerors through Him that loved us (Rom. 8:37). Thank You for Your plan for each of us and for this family! In Jesus's name, so be it.

A Prayer for Freedom From Fear

Father, in Jesus's name, we thank You that You have not given us the spirit of fear, but in its place we have the spirit of power—the Holy Spirit (Acts 1:8), the spirit of love—the Father, because God is love (1 John 4:8), and the spirit of a sound mind—Jesus, the Word of God (John 1:14), which transforms us and renews our minds (Rom. 12:2). We draw near to You, Lord. We resist the devil, and his fear, and he must flee from us now (James 4:7). We believe that Jesus took part in death for us, so that He might destroy him who had the power of death, that is, the devil. Because of Jesus we are delivered from the fear of death and the bondage that fear brings (Heb. 2:14–15).

We know we have been delivered out of the hand of our enemies, and we can serve the Lord today without fear (Luke 1:74). Therefore, no matter what we may face today, we refuse to fear. The Lord is our light and our salvation; whom shall we fear? The Lord is the strength of our lives; of whom shall we be afraid (Ps. 27:1)? We are established in righteousness, knowing our rights in Christ. We are far from oppression, for we shall not fear, and from terror, for it shall not come near us (Isa. 54:14). Even though they increase that trouble us, and many may rise up against us, we will lay down and sleep, for the Lord will sustain us. We will not be afraid of ten thousands of people who would set themselves against us round about (Ps. 3:1, 5–6).

When we lie down, we shall not be afraid, and our sleep will be sweet (Prov. 3:24). We believe God loves us as much as He loves Jesus (John 17:23), and His perfect love casts out all fear (1 John 4:18). The wicked flee when no one pursues them, but we are as bold as a lion (Prov. 28:1). We boldly say, "The Lord is our Helper, and we will not fear what man may do to us" (Heb. 13:6). We believe we dwell safely and shall be quiet from the fear of evil, because we listen to You (Prov. 1:33). Thank You, Lord, for total freedom from fear, in Jesus's name. Hallelujah!

A Prayer for Health and Healing

Father, in the name of Jesus, we come to You regarding this need, thanking You for healing. We praise You for what You have provided through Jesus Christ. Your Word says, "Surely He has borne our griefs—sickness, weakness, and distress—and carried our sorrows and pain…the chastisement needful to obtain peace and well-being for us was upon Him, and with the stripes that wounded Him we are healed and made whole" (Isa. 53:4–5, AMP).

You sent Your Word—Jesus—and healed us and delivered us from all our destructions (Ps. 107:20). As we attend to Your Word and let it not depart from our eyes and keep it in the midst of our hearts, it is life to us who find it and health and healing to our flesh (Prov. 4:21–22). According to Your Word, we believe we are healed. We realize and confess that healing has been given to us as a free gift, and we receive our healing in Jesus's name. Thank You that whosoever will, may come and freely drink of the water of life (Rev. 22:17). Jesus paid our debt for sickness and disease, and by His stripes we were healed (1 Pet. 2:24). Satan has no power over us any longer. We now walk free from sickness in Jesus's name. Amen. [Pray the scriptures below that address your specific need.]

Bones: "He keeps all his bones; not one of them is broken" (Ps. 34:20, AMP*).*

Deafness, blindness: "And in that day shall the deaf hear the words of the book, and the eyes of the blind shall see out of obscurity and out of darkness" (Isa. 29:18, KJV*).*

Eyesight: "And the eyes of them that see shall not be dim" (Isa. 32:3, KJV*).*

Heart: "My flesh and my heart faileth: but God is the strength of my heart, and my portion forever" (Ps. 73:26, KJV*).*

Blood poisoning: "I will cleanse their blood that I have not cleansed" (Joel 3:21, KJV*).*

Burns: "When you walk through the fire, you shall not be burned; nor shall the flame kindle on you" (Isa. 43:2, MEV*).*

Fatigue: "He gives strength to the weary, and to him who lacks might He increases power" (Isa. 40:29, NAS*).*

Bleeding, hemorrhaging: "When I passed by you and saw you rolling about in your blood, I said to you in your blood, Live!" (Ezek. 16:6, AMP*).*

Nerves: "And the peace of God, which passeth all understanding, shall keep your hearts and minds through Christ Jesus" (Phil. 4:7, KJV).

Speech impediment, stuttering: "The tongue of the stammerers will speak readily and plainly" (Isa. 32:4, AMP).

Teeth: "Your teeth are like a flock of sheep coming up from the washing. Each has its twin, not one of them is missing" (Song of Sol. 6:6, NIV).

Skin: "Let their flesh be renewed like a child's; let them be restored as in the days of their youth" (Job 33:25, NIV).

Stomach pain, food poisoning: "And ye shall serve the LORD your God, and He shall bless thy bread and thy water, and I will take sickness away from the midst of thee" (Exod. 23:25, KJV).

Learning disabilities: "In Him was life, and the life [the life of God] was the light of men [we walk in the light of eternal life]" (John 1:4). "We have the mind of Christ" (1 Cor. 2:16).

Miscarriage, barrenness: "There shall nothing cast their young, nor be barren, in thy land: the number of thy days I will fulfill" (Exod. 23:26, KJV).

Leukemia: "It [the Word] shall be health to your nerves and sinews, and marrow and moistening to your bones" (Prov. 3:8, AMP).

Protection from infectious disease: "No evil shall befall you, nor shall any plague come near your dwelling" (Ps. 91:10).

NOTES

Introduction

1. Tony Evans, *The Battle Is the Lord's*, (Chicago, IL: Moody Publishers, 2002), 73.

2. Maple Glen Church, "The Divine Design of Marriage, Part Two," May 5, 2013, http://mapleglenchurch.org/2013/08/sermon-the-divine-design-of-marriage-part-two-may-5-2013/ (accessed June 11, 2015).

Chapter 1—Your Spiritual Security System

1. John Phillips, *Bible Explorer's Guide: How to Understand and Interpret the Bible* (Grand Rapids, MI: Kregel Publications, 2002), 126.

2. Frank Seekins is an author and Bible teacher who has studied the word pictures created by studying the original Hebrew letters. Many of the Hebrew definitions I will share throughout this book are drawn from his teaching in *Hebrew Word Pictures* (Phoenix, AZ: Living Word Pictures, 1994).

3. Ibid, 138.

4. *Gan*, Strong's 1588, Blue Letter Bible Hebrew Lexicon, http://www.blueletterbible.org/lang/Lexicon/Lexicon.cfm?Strongs=H1588&t=KJV (accessed June 11, 2015); see also *ganan*, Strong's 1598, Biblesoft's New Exhaustive Strong's Numbers and Concordance with Expanded Greek-Hebrew Dictionary (Biblesoft and International Bible Translators, Inc., 1994).

Chapter 2—God's Design for Marriage

1. "Social Indicators of Marital Health and Well-Being," *The State of Our Unions*, http://www.stateofourunions.org/2012/social_indicators.php#divorce (accessed June 12, 2015).

2. National Center for Health Statistics, as quoted by Monica Watrous, "How Young Is Too Young?" McClatchy/Tribune News, May 15, 2010, http://www.chicagotribune.com/lifestyles/sc-fam-0513-young-married-20100513-story.html (accessed June 12, 2015).

3. DrPhil.com, "Marriage and Divorce: The Statistics," http://www.drphil.com/articles/article/351 (accessed June 12, 2015).

4. Ibid.

5. Shannon Philpott, "The Effect of Divorced Parents on a Child's Future Relationships," Mom.me, http://mom.me/parenting/6576-effect-divorced-parents-childs-future-relationships/ (accessed June 5, 2015).

6. Dr. Carolyn Leaf, *Who Switched Off My Brain* (Nashville, TN: Thomas Nelson, 2009).

7. *Adam*, Strong's 119, Blue Letter Bible., http://www.blueletterbible.org/lang/Lexicon/lexicon.cfm?Strongs=H119&t=KJV (accessed June 12, 2015).

8. "Genesis," *The Stone Edition of the Chumash* (Brooklyn, NY: Mesorah Publications, 1995), 13.

9. Shimon Apisdorf, "Operation 'Light' Up the World," Torah.org, http://www.torah.org/learning/basics/nutshell/part16.html (accessed June 12, 2015).

10. Ibid.

CHAPTER 3—THE KEY TO A HAPPY, LOVING MARRIAGE

1. Ezra, from Strong's 5826, Hebrew Lexicon, Blue Letter Bible, http://www.blueletterbible.org/lang/Lexicon/Lexicon.cfm?Strongs=H5830&t=KJV (accessed June 15, 2015).

2. Gesenius' Hebrew Chaldee Lexicon, H5048, *neged*, Blue Letter Bible, http://www.blueletterbible.org/lang/Lexicon/Lexicon.cfm?Strongs=H5048&t=KJV (accessed June 15, 2015).

3. Frank Seekins, *Hebrew Word Pictures* (Phoenix, AZ: Living Word Pictures, 1994), 143.

4. James Owen, "Men and Women Really Do See Things Differently," National Geographic News, September 6, 2012, http://news.nationalgeographic.com/news/2012/09/120907-men-women-see-differently-science-health-vision-sex/ (accessed June 15, 2015).

5. Mark Roth, "Some Women May See 100 Million Colors, Thanks to Their Genes," *Pittsburg Post-Gazette*, September 13, 2006, http://www.post-gazette.com/news/health/2006/09/13/Some-women-may-see-100-million-colors-thanks-to-their-genes/stories/200609130255 (accessed June 15, 2015).

6. *The Telegraph*, "Hunter Gatherer Brains Make Men and Women See Things Differently," July 30, 2009, http://www.telegraph.co.uk/news/uknews/5934226/Hunter-gatherer-brains-make-men-and-women-see-things-differently.html (accessed June 15, 2015) and Dr. Mehmet Oz, "Are Men and Women Different?"

Oprah.com, http://www.oprah.com/health/Are-Men-and-Women-Different_1/9 (accessed June 15, 2015).

7. Gregory L. Jantz, PhD, "Brain Differences Between Genders," *Psychology Today*, February 27, 2014, https://www.psychologytoday.com/blog/hope-relationships/201402/brain-differences-between-genders (accessed June 15, 2015).

8. Rabbi Benjamin Blech, *The Secrets of Hebrew Words* (Lanham, MD: Jason Aronson, 1977), 156.

9. Ibid.

10. Seekins, *Hebrew Word Pictures*, 138.

Chapter 4—Understanding His Needs

1. Joe S. McIlhaney and Freda McKissic Bush, *Hooked* (Chicago, IL: Northfield Publishing, 2008).

2. Ibid.

3. We have a CD teaching on this topic called *Pure Man*, which is available at kenblountministries.com. We also recommend *Every Man's Battle* by Steve Arterburn and Fred Stoeker and *Sex, Men, and God* by Douglas Weiss.

Chapter 5—Understanding Her Needs

1. Catherine Rampell, "U. S. Women on the Rise as Family Breadwinner," *New York Times*, May 29, 2013, http://www.nytimes.com/2013/05/30/business/economy/women-as-family-breadwinner-on-the-rise-study-says.html?_r=0 (accessed June 15, 2015).

2. Lauren Jacobs, "Why Strong, Independent Women Just Want to Be Taken Care of (Sometimes)," *Huffington Post*, November 12, 2013, http://www.huffingtonpost.com/lauren-jacobs/why-strong-independent-women-want-to-be-taken-care-of_b_3605582.html (accessed June 15, 2015).

3. "Hebrew Thoughts, Strong's 504," StudyLight.org, http://www.studylight.org/language-studies/hebrew-thoughts/?a=535 (accessed June 15, 2015).

4. Seekins, *Hebrew Word Pictures*; "The Basics of Life & Hebrew," El Shaddai Ministries, http://www.elshaddaiministries.us/messages/notes/5771/honor.pdf (accessed June 15, 2015); *Jewish Voice With Rabbi Jonathan Bernis*, December 17, 2012, http://www.itbn.org/index/detail/lib/people/sublib/Frank+Seekins/ec/Z5dXZ3Nzrq4DroOEwZ786_afkYmxFlcF (accessed June 15, 2015).

CHAPTER 6—THE POWER OF HONOR IN MARRIAGE

1. Blue Letter Bible Greek Lexicon, s. v. "*timē*," http://www.blueletterbible.org/lang/Lexicon/Lexicon.cfm?Strongs=G5092&t=KJV, (accessed June 18, 2015).

2. Gary Smalley and Norma Smalley, *Hidden Keys of a Loving, Lasting Marriage* (Grand Rapids, MI: Zondervan, 1993), 239.

CHAPTER 7—THE DEVIL IS ALWAYS AFTER THE SEED

1. Answersingenesis.org, "The Walls of Jericho," https://answersingenesis.org/archaeology/the-walls-of-jericho/ (accessed June 18, 2015).

2. Henry H. Halley, *Halley's Bible Handbook* (Grand Rapids, MI: Zondervan, 2008), 311

3. Need author to provide source information.

4. National Right to Life, "Abortion Statistics," http://www.nrlc.org/uploads/factsheets/FS01AbortionintheUS.pdf (accessed June 11, 2015).

5. Andrew Gibson, "Top Five US States' Population Growth: 2004–14," *Orlando Sentinel*, December 23, 2014, http://www.orlandosentinel.com/news/os-census-top-states-population-growth-htmlstory.html (accessed June 16, 2015).

6. Dan Brewster, "The '4/14 Window': Child Ministries and Mission Strategies," Compassion International, updated August 2005, http://www.compassion.com/multimedia/the%204_14%20Window.pdf (accessed June 11, 2015).

7. Barna Group, "Evangelism Is Most Effective Among Kids," October 11, 2004, https://www.barna.org/barna-update/article/5-barna-update/196-evangelism-is-most-effective-among-kids#.VXH4UdJViko (accessed June 15, 2015).

8. Jonathan Shooter, "The Past Is Our Future," http://www.torah.org/features/nextgen/pastfuture.html (accessed June 11, 2015).

CHAPTER 8—GOD CARES ABOUT CHILDREN

1. Rabbi Avrohom Chaim Feuer, *Tehillim/Psalms* (Brooklyn, NY: ArtScroll Mesorah Publications, 1996), 288; Nicholas Cachi, *The Image of the Good Shepherd as a Source for the Spirituality of the Ministerial Priesthood* (Rome, Italy: Gregorian University Press, 1995), 69–70.

2. Ravi Zacharias, *Can Man Live Without God* (Nashville, TN: Thomas Nelson, 2004), 26–27.
3. Ibid., 26.
4. Ibid., 23.

Chapter 9—A Blueprint for Building Strong Families

1. Unknown composer, "Shut In With God," www.smallchurchmusic3.com/Lyrics/D05/S05622.php (accessed June 15, 2015).
2. Feuer, *Tehillim/Psalms*.
3. American Life League, "Abortions in the United States," March 26, 2015, http://www.all.org/nav/index/heading/OQ/cat/MzQ/id/NjA3OQ/ (accessed June 20, 2015).
4. Children's Defense Fund, "The State of America's Children," http://www.childrensdefense.org/library/state-of-americas-children/2014-soac.pdf (accessed June 20, 2015).
5. Ibid.
6. Ibid.
7. Teen Mania Ministries, http://www.teenmania.com/about.html (accessed June 20, 2015).
8. "Family Structure," ChildTrends.org, http://www.childtrends.org/?indicators=family-structure (accessed June 20, 2015).
9. Dictionary.com, s.v. "train," http://dictionary.reference.com/browse/train?s=t (accessed June 20, 2015).

Chapter 10—Resisting the Culture

1. Lane Palmer, "You CAN Handle the Truth," *Christian Post*, May 12, 2006, http://m.christianpost.com/news/you-can-handle-the-truth-14091/ (accessed June 20, 2015).
2. Barna Group, "Most Twentysomethings Put Christianity on the Shelf Following Spiritually Active Teen Years," September 11, 2006, https://www.barna.org/barna-update/article/16-teensnext-gen/147-most-twentysomethings-put-christianity-on-the-shelf-following-spiritually-active-teen-years#.VXIU-tJViko (accessed June 20, 2015).
3. Claudia Wallis, "What Makes Teens Tick," *Time*, May 10, 2004, http://time.com/620/what-makes-teens-tick/ (accessed June 20, 2015).

4. Ibid.

5. See also *Talking to Your Kids About Sex* by Mark Lasser and *How and When to Tell Your Kids About Sex* by Stan Jones.

CHAPTER 11—INTRODUCING YOUR CHILDREN TO CHRIST

1. Our ministry has created several music CDs that teach children Bible verses and Bible stories. They can be found at kenblount ministries.com.

CHAPTER 12—BUILD A DYNASTY

1. Leah Kohn, "Shifrah and Puah/Miriam and Jochebed Part II," Torah.org, http://www.torah.org/learning/women/class46.html (accessed June 22, 2015); The Complete Jewish Bible With Rashi Commentary, Exodus 1:15, 20–21, http://www.chabad.org/library/bible_cdo/aid/9862#showrashi=true (accessed June 22, 2015).

ABOUT THE AUTHORS

THE HEARTBEAT OF Ken Blount Ministries (KBM) is helping the local church and its families connect with God. In a culture that often devalues family life and undermines God's design for marriage and parenting, KBM stands determined to provide families with the resources, the skills, and the spiritual support needed to go against the flow.

Ken and Trudi Blount have a background of thirty-plus years in ministry, and their godly wisdom, practical experience, and passion to see families succeed will inspire and equip you to raise up a strong family in this corrupt world.

For more information, visit
https://kenblountministries.com/.